Facing Blackness

Media and Minstrelsy in Spike Lee's *Bamboozled*

by Ashley Clark

Facing Blackness

Acknowledgments 5

Been Down a Long and Twisted Road:
A New Foreword for a New Edition 9

Original Foreword 17

Misrepresented People:
Bamboozled in Context 31

Dela Soulless:
Madness, Media, and the Mask 69

A Storm of Denigration:
The Horror of Minstrelsy 103

Bibliography 117

About the Author 127

Acknowledgments

I'd like to thank my mum, Helen, for nurturing my passion for cinema from a young age, and for encouraging me when I decided to attempt to parlay it into a career. I'd be nowhere without the backing and support from my family: my granddad Eddie aka "Popsicles" (1928–2017), who always made me believe that I could do anything I put my mind to; my dad Charles, who has enthusiastically shared my work far and wide; and my stepdad Simon, another film buff, who is responsible for my favorite ever line of film criticism, on Nick Love's *The Business* (2005): "It was good for 40 minutes, and then it just… *lost content.*" I owe a debt of gratitude to Ryan Gilbey, Danny Leigh and Geoff Andrew, who generously gave me tips on the film criticism game when I was starting out, and have remained supportive since. A laudatory word, too, for *Reverse Shot* co-founder and chief editor Michael Koresky—he is a kind and thoughtful man whose rigorous but sensitive editing helped me to become a far better writer. Thanks to Kaleem Aftab for providing advice and support, and for writing a truly invaluable official biography of Lee. I'd like to thank Ed Guerrero, the title of whose life-changing 1993 book *Framing Blackness: The African American Image in Film* I've rather cheekily referenced for my own effort. On this project I would have been stranded without the enthusiastic engagement and conversation of Jan Asante and Miriam Bale, who sent me countless links to features, articles and ephemera on subjects of race and representation.

It's my only regret that I couldn't fit all of this amazing information into the final manuscript. Additional thanks go to David Somerset, Brandon Harris, Eric Hynes, Jeff Reichert, Chris Wisniewski, Racquel J. Gates, Michael B. Gillespie, Charlotte Cook, Peter Becker, Liz Helfgott, Abbey Lustgarten, Gina Duncan, Jesse Trussell, Natalie Erazo, Jason Lampkin, Jake Perlin, Jim Colvill, and, of course, Spike Lee himself, for creating this haunting and deeply provocative work. Finally, the completion of this project would simply not have been possible without the love, patience, constant support, and extremely astute editorial feedback of Cathy Landicho Clark. She is an unbeatable companion, a constant inspiration, an amazing mother to Jasmine, and a formidable woman from a warm, welcoming family.

Been Down a Long and Twisted Road: A New Foreword for a New Edition

Less than two months before I submitted my final manuscript for the first edition of this book in 2015, one Donald J. Trump officially launched his bid to become President of the United States of America. I recall wondering whether I should reference Trump in the text. After all, *Bamboozled* was dedicated to Elia Kazan and Budd Schulberg's media satire *A Face in the Crowd* (1957), and Trump was a real-life Lonesome Rhodes, stretching the boundaries of parody and vulgarity in real time. I decided against it. Surely this Presidential run was nothing more than a baroque prank that could only end in crushing defeat for this satsuma-hued mountebank, reality TV star, and subliterate carnival barker who'd spent years wasting everyone's time by trying to prove that Barack Obama was Muslim?

Well, we all know how that went, and since then, American culture has turned up more than enough turbo-charged, upsetting tragedy and farce for *Bamboozled* to feel, if not tame by comparison, then even more horribly prescient than I'd feared.

As the national media landscape grew more furious, diffuse, polarized and impenetrable, real life started to become populated by characters and incidents that felt as though they'd come to ghoulish life from the *Bamboozled* cutting room floor. For just one example, consider prominent Trump acolytes Lynnette Hardaway and Rochelle Richardson, aka "Diamond and Silk," two black women who continue to profess their Trump adoration on video blogs, social media, and the right-wing extremist Newsmax channel.

Despite peddling, in the words of website *The Outline*, "a schtick so phony and lazily constructed that it could plausibly be an elaborate Dadaist prank," Diamond and Silk remain immensely popular, boasting over a million Twitter followers. If Pierre Delacroix had survived his assassin's bullet, and further jettisoned his soul, he simply could not have created a more egregious double act; the pair's cantankerous testimony before Congress at a 2018 hearing entitled "Filtering Practices of Social Media Platforms" simply must be seen to be believed. (Incidentally, I checked the pair's Twitter feed while writing this foreword, and found a tweet linking to a partnership video featuring larger-than-life conspiracy theorist and pillow magnate Mike Lindell. The deal? "Get up to 66% off right now when you Use Promo Code: TrumpWon.")

And what of Trump-supporting rapper/designer Kanye West, who dropped the following pearls of wisdom in a May 2018 interview with TMZ: "When you hear about slavery for 400 years ... For 400 years? That sounds like a choice. You were there for 400 years and it's all of y'all. It's like we're mentally imprisoned." Midway through *Bamboozled*, an increasingly misguided Delacroix makes eerily similar remarks in a radio interview with Imhotep Gary Byrd (a real-life DJ, playing himself): "Don't you people get it? We're in the 21st Century. Slavery was over four hundred years ago. All that stuff people talked in the old days, it's over. Folks always crying, white man this, white man that. Let's all grow up." West, who has only descended further into acute Fanonian crisis, is just one of a number of black American stars to have become mired in absurd, scarcely believable, one might say *Bamboozled*-esque controversy–Jussie Smollett with his tragicomic pretend-kidnap caper; Will Smith's Oscar slap heard round the world–with their racial identities pathologized for sport in the eyes of a rapacious media.

Bamboozled's fierce commentary on police brutality against black people came to feel even more resonant in the wake of shocking incidents, months apart in 2020, like the police killing of Breonna Taylor in Louisville, and the murder of George Floyd by a policeman in Minneapolis, which was filmed by the teenage bystander Darnella Frazier (who later won a Pulitzer Prize for her documenting efforts) and broadcast worldwide, lighting the fuse on the largest widespread uprisings in a generation. Further, bewildering tragedy struck in October 2020 when the actor Thomas Jefferson Byrd, so superbly unsettling in *Bamboozled* as the opportunistic MC Honeycutt, was murdered in Atlanta, Georgia at the age of 70.

While there is plenty to be bleak about, there's also some hope. In my original foreword, I cited one of *Bamboozled*'s key themes–the lack of opportunity for black filmmakers and TV creators to establish consistent careers making serious work—and lamented a general lack of progress since the release of Lee's film. One name I mentioned was Barry Jenkins, who was at that point stranded on one feature, 2008's *Medicine For Melancholy*. A year after the publication of my book, Jenkins's instant classic *Moonlight* (2016) won the Academy Award for Best Picture, and he has gone on to enjoy a prolific and influential career, not just as a director but as a producer and nurturer of new talent. And while there is space for vast industrial improvement and no room for complacency, as I write there seems to be an encouraging groundswell of black filmmakers making complex, personal and meaningful black stories, and an emerging generation of brilliant black journalists, thinkers and curators to amplify and contextualize them.

Strides have also been made in scorching, searching, black-authored satire, from Jordan Peele's already canonical, Oscar-winning expose of sham white liberalism *Get Out* (2017) and Donald Glover's remarkably protean FX series *Atlanta* (2016–), to Terence Nance and collaborators' extraordinarily dynamic HBO series *Random Acts of Flyness* (2018–), and the prickly provocations of comedian Ziwe, whose schtick mostly involves baiting overconfident white people into laying bare their cluelessness about their own racial privilege.

And, happily, *Bamboozled* itself has undergone something of a resurgence in the ensuing years. I'm at once too humble to take too much credit for this turn of events, and too vain not to assume at least some of the kudos. *Facing Blackness*'s release and subsequent series of supporting repertory screenings in 2015 (including one at the Brooklyn Academy of Music where I interviewed Lee onstage) did seem to prompt a not insignificant reawakening of interest in the film in some critical and audience circles, which was extremely heartening to me. In March 2020, the film, remastered and loaded with new special features, entered the Criterion Collection on Blu-ray and DVD, in the process finally becoming widely available once more after more than a decade of languishing out of print. I worked as a consulting producer on that release and wrote liner notes. Later that year, I joined Criterion as curatorial director.

In *Facing Blackness*, I declare that "*Bamboozled* is in fact the central work in Lee's canon—the house on fire to which all roads lead." Seven years on, I stand by that assessment, and Lee's most significant subsequent releases have explicitly harked back to *Bamboozled* more than any other of his films. Consider the wild, outsize sex and gun culture satire of *Chi-Raq* (2015), the expansive, unwieldy, violent revisionist war epic *Da 5 Bloods* (2020), or box office hit *BlacKkKlansman* (2018), which echoed *Bamboozled* in its sharply critical deployment of footage from *Gone With the Wind* and *The Birth of a Nation* to connect past national horrors to present ones. Lee won his first Oscar for *BlacKkKlansman* (for best original screenplay)–a long overdue accolade, for sure, but one which points to the more palatable nature of the film in contrast to its acrid, forbiddingly spiky, 2000 forebear.

It has been a pleasure to revisit the original text for this second edition, and I'm grateful to Jake Perlin and The Film Desk for the opportunity. Collectively, we agreed to retain the original foreword, which follows this one. I've also made a few minor additions, subtractions and tweaks to the main text–most notably in rearranging and re-integrating a number of footnotes which were unwisely hidden away as endnotes in the back of the first edition. I'm very happy with the end result. Thank you for reading.

Ashley Clark
June 2022

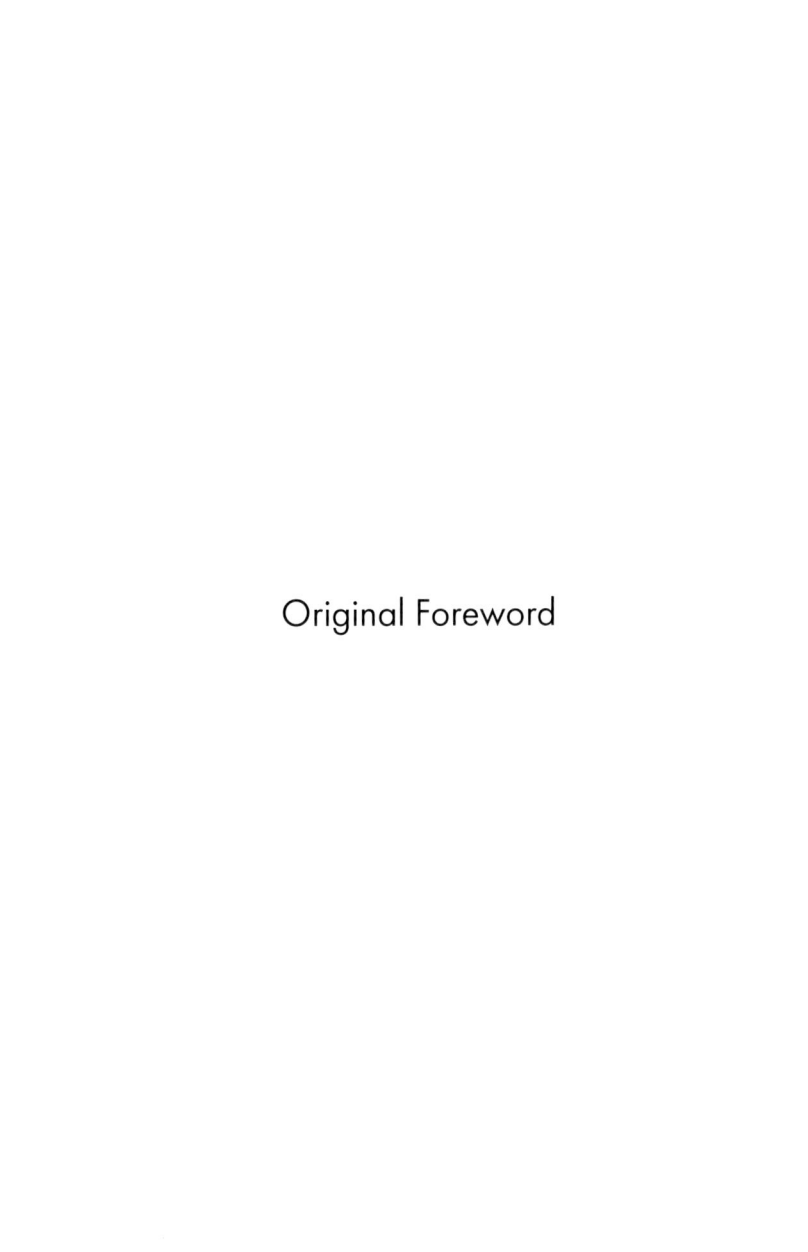

Original Foreword

I first saw *Bamboozled* as a 15-year-old, in April 2001, at the Ritzy Cinema in Brixton, Southwest London, and it threw me for a loop. Written and directed by Spike Lee, the film is an intense satire about a frustrated African American TV executive, Pierre Delacroix (Damon Wayans), who creates a contemporary version of a minstrel show in order to purposefully get himself fired, and expose the commissioning network as a racist and retrograde outfit. However, the show, which features its black stars wearing blackface, becomes a huge hit, prompting Delacroix's mental collapse, and an explosion of catastrophic violence, the effects of which are felt far and wide.

Even before attempting to process the film's challenging subject matter, I was confounded by its visual qualities. Much of *Bamboozled* was shot on consumer-grade, Mini DV digital video using the Sony VX 1000 camera, and later converted to the 35mm film format with jarringly murky results. It looked like nothing I'd ever seen on a big screen before—I remember earnestly wondering whether the projectionist had made a terrible mistake.

As a mixed-race British teenager with a limited understanding of American culture and history, I was left bewildered by its aggressively kaleidoscopic swirl of metamedia messages and specific reference points, from the sitcom *The Jeffersons* (1975-85), to the remarkably-coiffed civil rights campaigner Reverend Al Sharpton, to Bert Williams, a black Vaudevillian blackface performer.

I'd been dimly aware of the existence of a black and white minstrel show on the BBC (which I later discovered, to my astonishment, was canceled as late as 1978), but *Bamboozled*'s parade of grotesquery and debasement seemed a world away. More prosaically, I was either unable or unwilling to engage critically with its elliptical, choppy narrative, or its cacophonous late lurch into torrid romance and macabre melodrama.

Although I was profoundly emotionally disturbed by what I'd experienced, I was perhaps, in hindsight, afraid— or, to be more generous to myself, unprepared at that age— to delve into its deeper implications. I recall being quick in conversation with my mother (my viewing partner) to dismiss it as "messy and unfocused," pejoratives which have long been reflexively employed by critics to describe Lee's work. I looked to the mainstream-inclined *Empire* (my then film magazine of choice) for a second opinion, and sure enough, in a brief, two-star review, writer Kim Newman glibly waved it off as good "for Lee completists and tapdance junkies only." I was, to all intents and purposes, done with *Bamboozled*.

Yet over the years, as my tastes grew more adventurous and my critical faculties developed, I found that something about *Bamboozled* lodged in the back of my mind: blurry traces of its nightmarish plunge into psychological anguish; stubborn specks of its harrowing commentary on the pernicious presence of racism in mainstream entertainment.

Original Foreword

In December 2013, I read a feature on Lee by the *Guardian* columnist Gary Younge, in which he casually dismissed *Bamboozled* as "a dud." I had essentially done the same thing in 2001, but some 12 years later the judgment didn't sit right.

So, long overdue, I sat down once more with *Bamboozled*, this time on my laptop in a Starbucks tucked into a quiet corner of a sprawling New Jersey mall (the Garden State would soon become my permanent adopted home). I was, as the cliché goes, blown away: moved, on more than one occasion, to tears; and even angry at myself for failing to effectively engage with it previously.

As a youngster I'd seen an impenetrable tangle, but I now saw an invigoratingly experimental and deliberately diffuse work laced with heartfelt, honest expressions of confusion and fury. I was most struck by its steadfast rejection of a soothing narrative of progress in American entertainment and wider society. *Bamboozled* was effectively howling with gallows laughter at the utopian notion of a "post-racial society" eight years before the concept gained traction with the election of President Barack Obama.

In a fraught contemporary climate where the mediation of the black image in American society is at a crucial juncture, *Bamboozled*'s trenchant commentary on the importance, complexity and lasting effects of media representation could hardly feel more urgent. Each time an unarmed black person is killed, then hurriedly repositioned in death as a thug, a brute, or a layabout by mainstream media outlets—as has happened recently to Trayvon Martin, Michael Brown, Eric Garner, Samuel DuBose and countless others—we are seeing the perpetuation of old anti-black stereotypes, forged in the crucible of mass American art, reconfigured for our time. Lee's film traces a grim continuum between stereotypes old and new, connected by knotty skeins of institutional racism.

Many critics at the time of the film's release suggested that Lee had needlessly re-opened old wounds; that the dark days of minstrelsy were comfortably behind us, and that we should move on. Yet Lee's vision was not only necessary, it proved remarkably prescient. During the course of writing this book, I re-watched episodes of garish reality TV shows like *Flavor of Love* (2006-8), starring the clock-wearing rapper-cum-jester Flavor Flav, and *The Real Housewives of Atlanta* (2008-). I had to concede that *Bamboozled*'s nightmarish *New Millennium Minstrel Show* didn't look so far-fetched after all. I sat gape-mouthed in front of Lee Daniels and Danny Strong's musical soap opera *Empire* (2014-2020)—an entertaining but exceedingly dubious carnival of black pathologies—and couldn't help but wonder if it was the type of show that would get *Bamboozled*'s master-wigger network boss Dunwitty (Michael Rapaport) hot under the collar at proposal stage.

When, in October 2014, I saw footage of freshly-signed rapper Bobby Shmurda literally dancing on a table in front of a group executives, exactly like Manray (Savion Glover) does in *Bamboozled*, I began to wonder whether Lee was in fact a secret soothsayer. Not even he, however, could have predicted the transcendentally weird tale of Rachel Dolezal, the NAACP leader in Spokane, Washington, who was revealed to have been white, and posing as African American all along. At the time of the incident, many wags on social media suggested that Lee would be the ideal man to direct *Bamboozled 2: The Rachel Dolezal Story*.

Bamboozled's shrewd commentary on the lack of behind-the-scenes diversity in mainstream entertainment is also especially relevant today. The presence of figures like Robin Thede—head writer on *The Nightly Show with Larry Willmore*, and the first black woman to hold that position on a late night network comedy show—and Shonda Rhimes, the powerful showrunner behind *Grey's Anatomy*, *Scandal* and *How to Get Away with Murder*, is heartening. Yet a report released in March 2015 by the Writers Guild of America West revealed that minority writers accounted for just 13.7% of employment[1]: a dismal statistic. Moreover, Rhimes' success didn't insulate her from being disrespectfully branded as an "Angry Black Woman"—that most pernicious of stereotypes—in a supposedly flattering but rancid article by Alessandra Stanley in *The New York Times*.

---

1. The report is available to view in full at http://www.wga.org/uploadedFiles/who_we_are/tvstaffingbrief2015.pdf. [Accessed Aug 2, 2015].

While most of us[2] can cheer the incrementally increasing diversity on our film and television screens, *Bamboozled* forces us to question the quality and progressiveness of these roles. Ostensibly it's great that talented actors like Mo'Nique (*Precious*, 2009), Octavia Spencer (*The Help*, 2011) and Lupita Nyong'o (*12 Years a Slave*, 2013) are winning Oscars, but isn't the shine taken off somewhat by the fact they were rewarded by the establishment for playing, respectively, a psychotic "Welfare Queen," a neo-Mammy in a white savior period picture, and a chronically abused slave? Why don't black women win Oscars for playing complex heroines or crotchety geniuses like their white male counterparts? Because old stereotypes die hard within an industry that prefers stasis over change. Perhaps even more disturbingly, there's something inherently soothing about such stereotypes for mass audiences—a point particularly relevant to the wild popularity of *Bamboozled*'s own minstrel show.[3]

And how far have we come, really? Ridley Scott cast

---

2. I say "most of us," because I haven't forgotten "Pilots 2015: The Year of Ethnic Castings—About Time or Too Much of Good Thing?": a shockingly tone-deaf and frankly racist article by deadline.com writer Nellie Andreeva which left its skidmarks on the internet in March 2015.

3. Though *Bamboozled* restricts itself to issues around black representation, its lessons can be heeded elsewhere. Cheering news emerged in April 2015, when a group of Native American actors walked off the set of Adam Sandler comedy-western *Ridiculous 6* in protest at the demeaning roles they were being asked to play—they refused to be bamboozled.

a host of white actors (including a fake tan-enhanced Christian Bale and Joel Edgerton) in his Middle Eastern epic/flop *Exodus: Gods and Kings* (2014), but his response to complaints was both flippant, and distressingly matter-of-fact: "I can't mount a film of this budget, where I have to rely on tax rebates in Spain, and say that my lead actor is Mohammad so-and-so from such-and-such. I'm just not going to get it financed. So the question doesn't even come up." The best riposte to Scott and his film came from independent black filmmaker Terence Nance, who wrote that "like *The Birth of a Nation* before it, [*Exodus*] traffics in absurd cultural appropriation and brown-faced minstrel casting/make-up techniques to rewrite African history as European history, and in so doing propagates the idea that European cultural centrality is more important than historical fact and the ever-evolving self-image of African descended people as it is influenced by popular representations of people of color in Western media distributed worldwide."

Nance, however, is just one talented black filmmaker among many (Dee Rees, Tina Mabry, Haile Gerima, Julie Dash, Barry Jenkins et al.) who have struggled to attract funding to tell artistic and personal stories outside of the monolithic, corporate world of mainstream entertainment which *Bamboozled* so acidly depicts (even if it is set in the world of TV rather than film.) Lee has long been vocal about the struggles he faced in raising funds to tell black focused stories, and even he had to go cap in hand to fans on Kickstarter to crowdfund his idiosyncratic, low-budget vampire movie *Da Sweet Blood of Jesus* (2014). *Da Sweet Blood* is his most excessive, least easily readable work since *Bamboozled*, but it can't match his earlier film for sheer visceral impact.

Bamboozled, then, is a genuine one-off, but I can detect traces of its relentless, irritable, questioning approach in a variety of contemporary art. I see it in Justin Simien's tricky college-set satire *Dear White People* (2014), which was inspired by horrific, real-life blackface parties at universities across America.[4] I see it in the antic situational TV comedy of Keegan-Michael Key and Jordan Peele, whose best sketch, musical spoof "Negrotown" (2015), compresses the madness, pathos and insight of Lee's film into four-and-a-half harrowingly hilarious minutes. I see it in Branden Jacobs-Jenkins thrillingly audacious play *An Octoroon*

---

4. In the process of writing this book, I became aware of a number of disturbing incidents which proved that neither the phenomenon of blackface, nor the gratuitous indulgence of old stereotypes, has gone away. I was shocked to read that celebrity cook Paula Deen reportedly wanted black people to dress up as slaves at a wedding. More recently, I was horrified by the news that a fundraiser for the Baltimore cops charged in the April 2015 death of unarmed black man Freddie Gray would feature a blackface performance. I was also reminded by a friend that in 2010, on BBC comedy *Come Fly with Me*, British actor Matt Lucas had appeared in blackface, as a lazy, fat black woman called "Precious Little."

(2013), which reconfigures blackface tropes in daring ways. Most of all I see it coursing through the veins of Paul Beatty's scabrous satirical novel *The Sellout* (2015), about a young black Angeleno who hatches a plot to re-introduce racial segregation, and takes an elderly slave—a disturbed former "pickaninny" star of *Little Rascals* films—while he's at it. Like Lee's film, it plays as a shotgun blast to the face of formal convention, it's stubbornly resistant to a single concrete interpretation, and it has a lot of very painful things to say about America today.

ABC's enjoyably gentle sitcom *Black-ish* (2014-2022), meanwhile, simultaneously echoes Delacroix's crisis—with its premise of a middle-class black ad executive (Anthony Anderson) jockeying for position in a white corporate space—and feels like the kind of show Delacroix, free of Dunwitty's pressure, might have concocted himself.

Lastly, I couldn't help but think of *Bamboozled* while poring over Ta-Nehisi Coates' epic 2014 essay in *The Atlantic*, "The Case for Reparations," which uncovers, in forensic detail, the institutional plunder of black Americans from slavery to redlining to mass incarceration and its destructive impact on families. Coates' fury is more controlled than Lee's, but it's equally sincere, and his essay shares with *Bamboozled* the central imperative to look directly into the heart of past racial sins in order to plot a productive way forward.

It is time, then, to take a close look at *Bamboozled*, which deserves to be respected as much more than a mid-career oddity in Lee's filmography. It is a vital work that's equal parts crystal ball and cannonball: glittering and prophetic, heavy and dangerous.

Ashley Clark
August 2015

Misrepresented People: *Bamboozled* in Context

"As I begin to recognise that the Negro is the symbol of sin, I catch myself hating the Negro. But then I recognise that I am a Negro. There are two ways out of this conflict. Either I ask others to pay no attention to my skin, or else I want them to be aware of it. I try then to find value for what is bad—since I have unthinkingly conceded that the black man is the color of evil. In order to terminate this neurotic situation, in which I am compelled to choose an unhealthy, conflictual solution, fed on fantasies, hostile, inhuman in short, I have only one solution: to rise above this absurd drama that others have staged around me, to reject the two terms that are equally unacceptable, and through one human being, to reach out for the universal. When the Negro dives—in other words, goes under—something remarkable occurs."
—Frantz Fanon, *Black Skin, White Masks*

"Niggas is a beautiful thang."
—MC Honeycutt, *Bamboozled*

Born Shelton Jackson Lee in Atlanta, Georgia in 1957—but long famous as a part of New York's cultural firmament—Spike Lee has come to be regarded as the most prominent, prolific and controversial African American filmmaker working in the United States. Across a diverse career spanning more than three decades, Lee has operated in many genres, from musical to gritty drama, comedy to thriller. He's worked in fiction and documentary, and he's also well known for directing high-profile advertising campaigns—in 1997, Lee launched the advertising company Spike DDB. Although Lee's films often radically and thematically depart from one another, there are a few constants which bind them together: his engagement with sharply contested issues of identity, social power, and politics; his eschewal of hard realism for a heightened, cinematic style; his fondness for broad, voluble characters (some would say caricatures); and his dedication to depicting an informed, complex view of both historical and contemporary African American culture.

When people discuss their favorite Spike Lee "joint"—the name Lee uses for his own films—a few familiar titles tend to dominate the conversation. For some, his third film, the race relations-themed comedy-drama *Do The Right Thing* (1989), will forever be his masterpiece. It's a fizzing, fierce artistic achievement on its own terms, yet assumes an increasingly stately retrospective power whenever another unarmed black person—an Eric Garner; a Michael Brown; a Rekia Boyd; a Tamir Rice—is afforded the Radio Raheem treatment by the cops. For others it's his 1992 epic *Malcolm X*: that magnificent, continent-hopping monument to the eponymous activist, featuring a career-defining turn from Denzel Washington. A significant caucus plumps for the elegiac, post-9/11-set drama *25th Hour* (2002), which pop culture website *The A.V. Club* voted their second best film of the decade. The populist choice might be efficiently snappy heist/hostage thriller *Inside Man* (2006), which is one of his most easily digestible films, and comfortably his biggest box office success to date.[5] Still others suggest that Lee peaked outside the realm of narrative fiction with the 255-minute documentary *When The Levees Broke: A Requiem in Four Acts* (2006), an angry yet tender study of the aftermath of Hurricane Katrina.

His acrid take on race and the media, *Bamboozled*, by contrast, is hardly fan favorite material. It borrows its title from a portentous speech delivered by Denzel Washington-as-Malcolm X to his followers in Lee's biopic: "You've been hoodwinked. You've been had. You've been took. You've been led astray, led amok. You've been bamboozled"—a clear indication that the film's content will include confusion, compromise and ambiguity.

Even within the director's voluminous body of work—a prickly, decidedly American place in which confrontation comes as quickly and naturally as breathing—*Bamboozled* is an unwieldy, uncomfortable affair: a bleak treatise on the historically egregious misrepresentation of black people by the nation's corporate-entertainment complex; the devastating psychological and corporeal effects of this misrepresentation upon individuals; and the role that

---

5. All box office figures are sourced from http://www.boxofficemojo.com. *Inside Man* grossed $88,513,495 at the US box office, and almost $200m worldwide. Lee was still unable to find the funding to make a sequel.

we all, as active and passive consumers, play in it. Yes, *Bamboozled* is a self-described satire, but one ultimately ends up laughing at it in the same way one might laugh at a fatal clown car pileup: very quietly—if at all—with a fixed rictus born of guilt and gut-level terror.

* * *

Lee cited two major textual influences for *Bamboozled*, both prophetic media satires: Elia Kazan and Budd Schulberg's *A Face in the Crowd* (1957)—*Bamboozled* is dedicated to its writer Budd Schulberg, a close friend of Lee's—and Sidney Lumet and Paddy Chayefsky's *Network* (1976). The former tells the story of a boorish yet charismatic jailbird, "Lonesome" Rhodes (Andy Griffith), who makes the most of a lucky break to rise to televisual fame, jettisoning his integrity to become exceedingly rich along the way. The latter is a furious, freewheeling diagnosis of the blossoming cynicism of news television and its pernicious influence on dupe-like audiences. The mounting hysteria of these films, and their perceptive takes on mass media's aptitude for manipulating the public mood, are both clearly evident in *Bamboozled*. The films are also directly quoted: Rhodes' excitable catchphrase "Ooo-weee!" is lifted wholesale by MC Honeycutt (Thomas Jefferson Byrd), and a speech by *Network*'s mad prophet newscaster Howard Beale (Peter Finch) is reconfigured for a disturbing rant by performer

Misrepresented People: *Bamboozled* in Context

Manray (Savion Glover) in character as "Mantan" in the show's pilot episode. The murder of Manray by a radical rap group named the Mau Maus, meanwhile, is a clear echo of the slaying of Beale by the Ecumenical Liberation Army, *Network*'s own haphazard gaggle of bad tempered militants.

Bamboozled also has roots in one of Lee's first-year projects at New York University film school. In 1980, aged 23, he wrote and directed a 20 minute satire entitled *The Answer*[6], about an out-of-work black screenwriter who agrees to pen a remake of D. W. Griffith's notoriously racist epic *The Birth of a Nation* (1915) for $50 million. Before selling his soul—and effectively going the way of Delacroix—the screenwriter decides that he cannot go through with it; even so, he is attacked by Klan members, who burn a cross in front of his house. Of being taught *The Birth of a Nation* at NYU, Lee told *The Guardian*'s John Colapinto: "They talk about all the 'innovations' ... But they never really talked about the implications of [it], never really talked about how that film was used as a recruiting tool for the KKK." *The Answer* incensed some NYU faculty members, who recommended Lee's expulsion from the

---

6. Justin Simien's *Dear White People* (2014) features a clear nod to Spike Lee's experience of making *The Answer* at NYU. In an early scene, one of the central characters, radical film student Sam (Tessa Thompson), screens her short film *The Rebirth of a Nation*. It features white people in whiteface berating Barack Obama, and it frightens her classmates into silence.

program. Lee was ultimately allowed to remain, but even the more supportive responses of some staff betrayed irritation at this young tyro's contradiction of the canon. Eleanor Hamerow, former head of the department, told *The Guardian* in 2009: "He was trying to solve a problem overnight—the social problem with the blacks and the whites. He undertook to fix the great film-maker who made that movie, D. W. Griffith." How dare he?

Bamboozled was not the first film to harness blackface imagery in complex and provocative ways in the period long after the practice was widely deemed unacceptable. Carl Lerner's *Black Like Me* (1964) told the curious-but-true story of a white Texan journalist, John Howard Griffin, who spent six weeks traveling throughout the racially segregated south with darkened skin in an attempt to comprehend the lived experiences of black people. (This earnest social experiment was given a frantic comic spin in Melvin Van Peebles's wacky comedy *Watermelon Man* [1970], which stars black actor Godfrey Cambridge–initially in heavy make-up–as a racist white man who wakes up one day to suddenly discover he's become black; and later flipped on its head in the classic satirical *Saturday Night Live* sketch *White Like Me* [1984], in which Eddie Murphy, in Godfrey Cambridge-esque whiteface make-up, goes undercover in white New York society: he is shocked to see the many privileges and benefits he receives, from a cocktail party on a city bus to free money at the bank.)

Misrepresented People: *Bamboozled* in Context

In a wildly different register, Brian De Palma's *Hi, Mom!* (1970) digressed from its main narrative to present "Be Black, Baby!," a thrillingly anarchic mock-documentary of an immersive theatrical experience, in which a group of black actors in whiteface show an audience of right-on, blacked-up WASPs what it's really like to be a black urbanite, with cataclysmic, shockingly funny results. The infamous, glaringly misguided comedy *Soul Man* (1986), meanwhile, starred C. Thomas Howell as a pampered preppy who blacks up to take advantage of a minorities-only program at Harvard.[7] Its satire is toothless enough to make Ben Stiller's cozy Hollywood industry in-joke *Tropic Thunder* (2008)—in which Robert Downey Jr. dons blackface to play a pompous method actor, while the film's only actual black star Brandon T. Jackson languishes in a cartoonish supporting role—look radical.

Much more successful was Robert Townsend's *Hollywood Shuffle* (1987), a sharp satire on the limited roles available for black actors in a supposedly more enlightened era. In one of its best scenes, white movie execs repeatedly demand an "Eddie Murphy type," while the camera pans across a row

---

7. In a scarcely-believable instance of life imitating art, Vijay Chokalingam—the brother of comedian Mindy Kaling—revealed in April 2015 that, as an undergraduate at the University of Chicago, he applied to medical school claiming to be African American, believing that it would "dramatically enhance" the chances of his success. He had mediocre grades and only received one offer, even while posing as black.

of bare-necked, leather-jacketed black actors, the lighter-skinned of whom wear blackface make-up out of pure desperation. Our hero, Bobby Taylor (Townsend), tries to protest, but he reflexively bursts into an impression of the famed comedian's trademark cackle. *Hollywood Shuffle* is a good-natured film, but its subject matter, and this nightmarish sequence, make it a clear forerunner for *Bamboozled*.

* * *

Lee wastes no time in broaching weighty themes in *Bamboozled*'s opening moments. Things kick off in baroque fashion with the anachronistic sound of a harpsichord—accompanied by the flap of bird wings, the creaking of a (slave?) ship and lapping waves—trilling over a black screen for a few moments. The logo of studio New Line appears, and the instantly recognizable vocals of Stevie Wonder join the mix. He sings:

> In 1492 you came upon these shores.
> Seven hundred years, educated by the moors;
> 17th Century—genocide and the gun
> Middle Passage blessed to market the Africans.
> In the so-called 'Land of God'
> My kind were treated hard
> From back then until now
> I see, and you agree—
> We have been a misrepresented people.

Misrepresented People: *Bamboozled* in Context

The lyrics to "Misrepresented People" are not ambiguous, and the song's switch to a mode of direct address ("I see, and you agree") acts as a deliberately confrontational implication of the viewer. This imposition of sociohistorical material chimes with the director's penchant for messaging during opening credit sequences, with the effect of instantly embedding the imminent narrative within a wider context.

This choice recalls a number of classic Lee openings, like the collage of imagery—from slave ship diagrams to Marcus Garvey, Willie Mays to Martin Luther King—which eases us into college-set musical comedy *School Daze* (1988); the first few seconds of *Do The Right Thing*, in which a brief instrumental rendition of the Negro hymn "Lift Every Voice and Sing" (aka the Black National Anthem) segues into the blazing clarion call of Public Enemy's rap classic "Fight the Power"; or, most memorably, the extraordinary opening montage in *Malcolm X*, which interweaves genuine footage of the infamous LAPD police beating of Rodney King in 1991, an image of the American flag burning into the shape of an X, and a voiceover of Washington-as-Malcolm delivering an incantatory speech directly addressed to black Americans: "I charge the white man with being the greatest murderer on earth. I charge the white man with being the greatest kidnapper on earth … You are one of 22 million black people who are the victims of America."

Bamboozled then transports us into the tortured sphere of the pompous Delacroix, an executive at CNS—a failing (and fictional) television network based in Manhattan. He's under pressure to deliver ratings, but is chronically frustrated by the lack of opportunities he is given by his asinine, wannabe-black boss Thomas Dunwitty (Michael Rapaport) to create shows for and about middle-class African Americans. Dunwitty tells him that the days of *The Cosby Show*—and other "safe," middlebrow, aspirational black sitcoms, like Delacroix's own canceled prior effort, the unpromising-sounding *Brown Nose Jones*—are stone dead. Delacroix believes, not without reason, that the network only wants to see black people represented as buffoons.

In order to expose the ingrained racism of the network, Delacroix, reluctantly backed by his recently-installed assistant Sloan (Jada Pinkett Smith), proposes the most offensive idea he can conjure, "a coon show—something so negative, so offensive and so racist that it will prove my point." This turns out to be a would-be satirical, modern-day minstrel show starring two impoverished, homeless black buskers—Manray and Womack (Tommy Davidson), whom Delacroix tempts with the promise of big money. It's a bold pitch, plunging deep into the dark depths of American cultural history.

The blackface minstrel show first emerged in the United States in the pre-Civil War era, and is widely recognized, but rarely celebrated, as the nation's inaugural indigenous theatrical artform. One of its first proponents was Thomas Dartmouth "Daddy" Rice, a struggling white actor who in 1828 found fame by impersonating a disabled black person—historians have debated whether his inspiration was a slave or a stable boy. Rice took the song that the black man was allegedly singing, "Jump Jim Crow," allied it with an exaggerated performance, blacked up his face, and remodeled himself with great success and influence as an "Ethiopian Delineator." Proving that popular culture has always been a matter of great importance, rather than a trifling distraction from "real" issues, the song's name ultimately came to be used as the catch-all title for the discriminatory "Jim Crow" laws in America's Southern states which arose after Reconstruction ended in 1877, and continued until their legislative dismantling, prompted by the civil rights movement, in the mid-1960s.

After archly and quickly regaling Dunwitty with some strictly top-line—and slightly wobbly—minstrel history[8] ("it began in the 1840s ... a variety show in which the talent was singing, dancing, telling jokes and doing skits... like *In*

---

8. For complementary, comprehensive studies of the birth, maintenance and development of negative racial stereotypes of African Americans in theater, film and television, I strongly recommend the book *Toms, Coons, Mulattoes, Mammies and Bucks* by Donald Bogle and the sober, cogently argued essay films *Ethnic Notions* (1986) and *Color Adjustment* (1991) by the brilliant, and sadly late, documentarian Marlon Riggs.

Living Color"[9]), and establishing that the show should revive and include old-school racist stereotypes like "Rastus, Little Nigger Jim, Sambo and Aunt Jemima," Delacroix suggests that it could take place in the contemporary projects. Dunwitty ups the stakes to suggest an antebellum plantation setting. Sloan, perhaps not expecting Delacroix to follow through so thoroughly on his promise, wonders aloud whether her colleague has lost his mind—but he goes even further to propose that it should be set on a watermelon patch. As per William Black in *The Atlantic*, this particularly offensive trope "came into full force when slaves won their emancipation during the Civil War. Free black people grew, ate, and sold watermelons, and in doing so made the fruit a symbol of their freedom. Southern whites, threatened by blacks' newfound freedom, responded by making the fruit a symbol of black people's perceived uncleanliness, laziness, childishness, and unwanted public presence. This racist trope then exploded in American popular culture, becoming so pervasive that its historical origin became obscure."

---

9. Writing in the *Village Voice*, Amy Taubin interpreted this reference to the Fox comedy sketch show as a barb directed at Wayans and Davidson, who both starred in it. Lee was not amused. In his DVD commentary, he says: "Taubin wrote that I cast Damon and Tommy to get back at a show that's been off the air for ten years. Now where in the fuck did she get that from? She never interviewed me, she never asked me. I called her up and cursed her ass out. She said 'Well I thought … I read somewhere …' I said 'You ain't read a motherfucking thing. I never said that I did not like *In Living Color*.'"

Misrepresented People: *Bamboozled* in Context

It's left to an emboldened Dunwitty to complete this absurd game of one upmanship when he beamingly announces that the stars of the show should appear in burnt-cork blackface—a tradition that was largely eliminated from American film comedy after the end of the 1930s, when it became harder to defend as innocuous, and more increasingly associated with racism and bigotry.

Delacroix casually renames Manray to "Mantan" (a reference to Mantan Moreland, a black performer popular in the 1930s and 40s[10]) and Womack to "Sleep n' Eat" (after the stage name of Willie Best, a black actor, also prolific in the 30s and 40s, famed for playing stereotypically lazy, illiterate, and/or simple-minded characters). He declares that they will be "two real coons," a moniker that was adopted in 1896 by real-life black performing duo Bert Williams and George Walker in order to help them secure work with white clients—Williams, the sad clown of the pair, wore blackface; Walker, the straight man, did not. The quiet horror of this exchange is intensified by the boardroom presence of the two performers who, initially at least, look on in silent confusion, consigned to

---

10. The choice of this name has proved contentious among some critics. Donald Bogle has argued that the film overlooks an important aspect of Mantan's career, namely "that, as the star of [independent black] 'race' movies, including *Mantan Runs for Mayor* (1946) and *Mantan Messes Up* (1946), Moreland clearly had a black following that didn't see him as a sellout."

stereotypes before they can blink. Womack is skeptical, though Manray becomes more enthusiastic. In a display of alarming eagerness, he leaps onto the table to tap dance for his potential new bosses. Delacroix figures that if the show is somehow commissioned, its inevitable failure will lead to the termination of his contract, a handsome severance package, and the public shaming of CNS.

Sloan receives a visit at her Brooklyn home from her brother Big Blak Afrika (Mos Def), who heads up a shambolic collective of revolutionary rappers named the Mau Maus, who are named after an anti-colonialist uprising in Kenya that took place between 1952 and 1960. He wants Sloan to help them secure a spot on the putative show, but she's having none of it. He becomes irritated at Sloan for calling him by his birth name, Julius: "You don't call El Hajj Malik El Shabazz [Malcolm X] Detroit Red," he complains. On one hand, he makes a cogent point about the importance of recognizing one's self-determined identity, and the history of African Americans disassociating themselves from former slave names; on the other, he's comparing himself to Malcolm X—the first sign that he's not quite living in the real world.

In a hilarious montage sequence, Delacroix and Sloan audition acts for supporting roles on the show. Indicating that he has some awareness of the predicament for black performers outside of his own pampered, hermetic universe, Delacroix comments drily and ruefully on the surprising volume of hopefuls in attendance: "One small ad in *Backstage* had Negroes lined up around the block." He's keen on the loquacious orator Honeycutt (Thomas Jefferson Byrd) and band The Alabama Porch Monkeys (played by real life conscious hip-hop act The Roots), but he's less impressed by an obese soul singer (Tuffy Questell), who hollers a revoltingly misogynistic number ("I be smackin' dem hoes!"), and the Mau Maus. After witnessing their intemperate performance, he sniffs "I don't want to have anything to do with anything black for at least a week."

Delacroix assumes he'll have full authorial control over the show, but his flimsy plan soon begins to unravel. Dunwitty surprises and enrages him by drafting in a twenty something Finnish tyro with a shock of white hair (Jani Blom) to helm the pilot and redraft the script. In one of the film's most bitterly ironic jokes, it becomes clear that Delacroix will not even be permitted to serve as the author of his own downfall. The pilot, which revolves around Manray delivering a jeremiad about being "sick and tired of niggers," before passing out and being woken up by the smell of watermelon, draws a decidedly mixed response from a multiracial, multiethnic studio audience. The CNS top brass, however, like what they see, and order a full series as a mid-season replacement for another show.

Lee briefly sweetens the film's vinegary tone for a poignant, humane scene in which Delacroix, who seems to be suffering from an attack of conscience, pays a visit

Facing Blackness

to his father Junebug (Paul Mooney), a veteran Chitlin' Circuit[11]-style comedian who works blue for appreciative black audiences in small nightclubs. Though Junebug is ostensibly happy, he's also a boozehound living job-to-job. Delacroix resolves not to end up like his father, so redoubles his commitment to what has now been titled *Mantan: The New Millennium Minstrel Show*.

In a twist informed by *The Producers'* "Springtime for Hitler" farrago[12], the actual show—which comes to resemble a modern, foul-mouthed spin on more traditional minstrel revue performances, with Mantan and Sleep n' Eat performing comedy and dance routines—is rapaciously consumed by audiences across America, who fall for its energetic evocation of bygone racist stereotypes. What's more, the blackface sported by its stars (and studio spectators) becomes a youth craze like the yoyo or Pokémon before it. The show also, however, inspires a severe backlash in some black media and activist circles.

---

11. The "Chitlin' Circuit" was the collective name given to a series of black-owned nightclubs, dance halls, juke joints and theaters that were safe and acceptable for African American entertainers to perform in during segregation.

12. *Springtime for Hitler: A Gay Romp With Eva and Adolf at Berchtesgaden* is a fictional musical about Adolf Hitler in Mel Brooks' film *The Producers* (1967). It's chosen by the producer Max Bialystock and his accountant Leo Bloom in their fraudulent scheme to raise funding by selling 25,000% of a play, causing it to fail, and keeping all of the remaining money for themselves. It is, of course, a runaway success.

Misrepresented People: *Bamboozled* in Context

Dunwitty brings in a patronizing PR consultant, Myrna Goldfarb (Dina Pearlman), who outlines a glib and incoherent strategy to deal with any controversy the show may spark. She flaunts her right-on credentials by announcing that she has a PhD in African American studies from Yale, and that her parents marched with Dr. Martin Luther King in Selma in 1965. Delacroix and Sloan are far from impressed.

Delacroix subsequently becomes torn between seduction by his newfound success and an increasingly visceral self-loathing: his psychological stress is connoted by the chilling and mysterious accumulation of collectible racist memorabilia in his office. One figurine, a cash-collecting "jolly nigger bank," pointedly donated to him by Sloan, seems to develop a life of its own.

Womack walks away from the show after deciding he can no longer endure the shame of blacking up, nor can he stomach working with Manray, who acts in an increasingly diva-ish manner. Manray, for a time, luxuriates happily in his new material wealth, and embarks on a tentative romance with Sloan. This infuriates Delacroix, who urges Manray to stop seeing her. He tells Manray that he once had a relationship with her, and that she slept with him to win her role at CNS.[13] Manray confronts Sloan, and soon after

---

13. The romantic subplot is abrupt and dramatically unsatisfying: it's certainly the film's least successful element. Deleted scenes included on the DVD further develop the relationship between Sloan and

Facing Blackness

also decides to quit the show, despite frantic protestations from Delacroix, who is terrified of alienating his corporate paymasters. Manray performs a liberating dance, with no blackface or costume, in front of a shocked and dismayed audience, before he's bundled out of the studio by security.

Sadly, Manray's moral ascension only slightly precedes his kidnap by the Mau Maus, who have grown increasingly agitated by the show and its runaway popularity. Branding him a disgrace to the race, they force him to tap-dance at gunpoint, then broadcast his execution-by-gunfire live on the internet. (This is, the viewer will note, an extremely prescient foreshadowing of the grimly innovative online techniques that would come to be used by terror outfit ISIS to disseminate images of death and torture.) The entire Mau Mau squad, save for its sole white member, the optimistically-named One-Sixteenth Blak (MC Serch), are

---

Manray, but it's hard to argue that the film, which runs to 136 minutes, would benefit from being any longer. That said, a more carefully-drawn portrayal of her relationship with Manray would certainly have afforded her final scene greater emotional ballast. Regarding the character of Sloan: while I take issue with Armond White's ad hominem attacks on the film and Lee in general in his *New York Press* review "More Trash by Spike Lee," he is justified in his bafflement over the characterization of Sloan. He writes that "[h]er inconsistency is mind boggling. Patronizing, too. When Manray accuses Sloan of sleeping her way up the network ladder, she bluffs with feminist rage— either Lee or Pinkett Smith wants to ignore the damning detail that she did indeed sell her assets."

Misrepresented People: *Bamboozled* in Context

then summarily massacred by the police. This depiction of disproportionate brutality toward people of color is a direct reference to the NYPD's similarly horrific treatment of black men like the Haitian Abner Louima, who was assaulted, brutalized and forcibly sodomized with a broken-off broom handle by officers after being arrested outside a Brooklyn nightclub in 1997; and Amadou Diallo, an unarmed Guinean immigrant who was killed after being shot at 41 times in 1999. One-Sixteenth begs the cops to kill him too, but he is saved by dint of his skin color.

A devastated, gun-toting Sloan, who has suddenly lost her brother and her lover, visits Delacroix in his apartment. He has smashed up all of his figurines, and is himself wearing blackface make-up: a gesture pitched somewhere between shame-induced self-abasement and outright psychosis. She blames him for the chaos, and shoots him in the gut. She inserts a VHS tape that she had earlier donated to him—but that he had neglected to watch—and tells him: "Look at what you've contributed to." He bleeds out while watching the tape: it is a grueling, three-minute montage comprising genuine footage of American entertainment's most offensive historical images, including blacked-up Hollywood stars like Judy Garland, Mickey Rooney, and Eddie Cantor; a number of black stars in demeaning "coon" and "mammy"[14] roles (Stepin Fetchit,

---

14. As Marlon Riggs's film *Ethnic Notions* (1986) argues, from slavery through the Jim Crow era, the "mammy" image served the political,

Butterfly McQueen); racist cartoons; and disturbing scenes from films like *The Birth of a Nation* (1915)[15] and Victor Fleming's much-loved plantation romance *Gone With The Wind* (1939).

Lee fills the screen with this montage, so the viewer effectively assumes the point-of-view of the dying Delacroix, who exhibits a degree of self-awareness in a poignant voiceover: "As I bled to death, as my very life oozed out of me, all I could think of was something that the great Negro James Baldwin had written: 'People pay for what they do, and still more for what they have allowed themselves to become, and they pay for it very simply by the lives they lead.' Maybe Baldwin was right, maybe he

---

social, and economic interests of mainstream white America. During slavery, the mammy caricature was posited as proof that blacks—in this case, black women—were contented, even happy, as slaves. Her wide grin, hearty laughter, and loyal servitude were offered as evidence of the supposed humanity of the institution of slavery. The "coon" caricature is one of the most insulting of all anti-black caricatures. The name itself, an abbreviation of raccoon, is dehumanizing. Like the "sambo," the coon was portrayed as a lazy, easily frightened, chronically idle, inarticulate, buffoon.

15. *The Birth of a Nation* is well-regarded for its technical and narrative innovations, but it is also shockingly racist. It recasts the Reconstruction period as a time of terror, with blacked-up white actors playing a barbaric militia (supported by the conquering white northerners) preying on terrified southern whites. Then-President Woodrow Wilson is reported as saying of the film: "It is like writing history with lightning, and my only regret is that it is all so terribly true."

was wrong. But as my father often told me, always keep 'em laughing."[16]

That final equivocation is devastating, because it underlines the persistence of the mask and the fixed grin as a method of maintenance for black people in entertainment. It doesn't save Delacroix, and it doesn't save Manray, who is briefly revived, as Mantan, in the film's desperately chilling final image: a close-up of his smiling, sweating face, slathered and trapped in that glistening burnt cork and fire engine-red lipstick. The sound of a cheering offscreen crowd escalates while the image is held for an uncomfortably long time, then: a cut to black, and he's gone forever.

In one last yank on the emotional lever, Lee runs the closing credits over haunting images of collectible racist memorabilia—a gut-wrenching parade of smiling, thick-lipped sambo dolls and Aunt Jemima figurines, floating serenely yet menacingly toward and away from the camera[17]. It's soundtracked by Bruce Hornsby's doleful ballad "Shadowland," which speaks eloquently to the film's

---

16. The quote is taken from James Baldwin's 1972 book *No Name in the Street*.

17. This visual strategy is remarkably similar to one used by Marlon Riggs in *Ethnic Notions*, though I can find no record of a direct acknowledgment from Lee. Previously, Riggs' documentary *Tongues Untied* (1989) strongly critiqued Lee's *School Daze* (1988) for its use of homophobic tropes.

themes of self-sabotage, self-loathing and solitude: "Been down a long and twisted road / Sensing myself at a record low / Do anything just to get ahead / Now it's all quiet here in this Shadowland."

* * *

According to Lee's official biographer Kaleem Aftab, *Bamboozled* had been brewing within the director for some years, and it was the film in which he would allow years of frustration with the industry—including a traumatic experience funding and making *Malcolm X*[18]; his failure to get a number of passion projects, like a mooted biopic of Jackie Robinson, off the ground; and a stream of controversies linked to his outspoken public persona[19]—to boil over.

---

18. The bond company which kept the film afloat in post-production folded, so Lee plowed $2m of his own $3m fee into the movie. Ultimately, Lee had to call upon a generous, moneyed black talent pool (including Oprah Winfrey, Janet Jackson, Bill Cosby, Tracy Chapman and Prince) for help. Lee recorded the production process in a bitterly funny book, *By Any Means Necessary: the Trials and Tribulations of Making Malcolm X* (tellingly subtitled *While 10 Million Motherfuckers Are Fucking with You!*).

19. Examples of the media painting Lee as a stereotyped "angry black man" are too numerous to list here, but perhaps the most egregious was an October 1992 interview by Barbara Grizzuti Harrison in *Esquire* magazine, which ran with the ridiculously inflammatory headline, "Spike Lee Hates Your Cracker Ass."

Misrepresented People: Bamboozled in Context

In interviews pegged to the film's release, Lee spoke ominously of a contemporary media machine eager to reconfigure old negative racial stereotypes into new forms of "neo-minstrelsy," particularly in the arenas of gangsta rap, mainstream filmmaking and television programming. He specifically cited the ludicrous portrayal of black characters in dismal sitcoms like the self-explanatory *Homeboys in Outer Space* (1996-7) and the inexplicable, slavery-themed lark *The Secret Diary of Desmond Pfeiffer* (1998), both of which aired on the UPN network. Lee also referred to Jar Jar Binks—the subservient, jive-talkin' cod-Jamaican alien in *Star Wars Episode 1: The Phantom Menace* (1999)—as "the science fiction Stepin Fetchit."

He later railed in his *Bamboozled* DVD commentary against retrograde roles for the black stars of Hollywood hits *The Green Mile* (1999) and *The Legend of Bagger Vance* (2000): "Michael Duncan Clarke [sic] ... has the power to touch Tom Hanks and cure him of his illness, but he can't get himself out of jail! [Bagger] Vance has magical mystery powers but maybe he could stop one or two people from getting lynched down there in Georgia!" Lee told *Cineaste*'s Gary Crowdus and Dan Georgatos that Will Smith turned down the role of Delacroix in order to play Bagger Vance.

The director also had harsh words for actors whom he perceived to be shucking and jiving for acceptance by the Hollywood establishment, including Cuba Gooding Jr., whose "Show Me The Money" Oscar acceptance speech in

1997 perhaps featured more dancing and prancing than it ought to have done; and Ving Rhames, who made a well-intentioned but bizarre spectacle of donating his Golden Globe award to Jack Lemmon at the 1998 ceremony. Both of these incidents are explicitly referenced late in *Bamboozled*, when Delacroix has a bitterly funny, prelude-to-death daydream—featuring cameos from Mira Sorvino and Matthew Modine—about being accepted by the industry elite.

Lee also brought up the question of choice in interviews: "My people have to wake up and realize what's going on and our responsibility in it," he told *Newsweek*'s Allison Samuels, making his position unequivocally clear. "I mean, back in the day we didn't have a choice. Hattie McDaniel and Bill "Bojangles" Robinson didn't have a choice. Nowadays we don't have to do this stuff." Lee would later, in 2009, famously accuse the producer, actor and director Tyler Perry—whose down-home comedic work is wildly popular with mainstream African American audiences—of indulging in "coonery and buffoonery."

* * *

Despite its eclectic mixture of influences, topical subject matter and palpable passion, *Bamboozled* proved too bitter a pill for most audiences to swallow. It was released in American cinemas on October 6, 2000, and grossed a meager

$2,274,979 against a budget of $10m. Lee told Aftab that he blamed the studio New Line for its failure, stating "[t]hey didn't believe in the film, so there was no investment beyond the initial one." As *Reverse Shot*'s Michael Koresky observes, it was unlikely that the Time Warner-owned company were ever going to "put their hearts, souls, and cash behind a film that meant to call out the rancid stereotyping of African Americans, past, present, and (gulp) future." The influential *New York Times* also refused to run an advertisement for the film that featured a "pickaninny" caricature of a black child and a watermelon, claiming it was too offensive.

Of Lee's twenty-plus films to secure theatrical release in America to date, only dubious lesbian-impregnation comedy-drama *She Hate Me* (2004), micro-budget experimental drama *Red Hook Summer* (2012), and limp action remake *Oldboy* (2013) have fared worse in financial terms. In an ironic twist, the film Lee released months earlier in 2000, *The Original Kings of Comedy*—a documentary record of four African American stand-up comics doing largely risqué material specifically catered to black audiences—cleaned up at American theaters, grossing $38,182,790.[20]

Aside from more obvious reasons, like its controversial subject matter and conspicuous deficit of likable characters,

---

20. There is no box office data available for 2014's *Da Sweet Blood of Jesus*, which premiered on streaming site Vimeo and had a very limited theatrical release in February 2015.

one explanation for the magnitude of *Bamboozled*'s failure was its reception from prominent American critics. Even the positive reviews were qualified, though they recognized the film's cultural significance. "In going where few have dared to tread, *Bamboozled* is an almost oxymoronic entity, an important Hollywood movie," wrote Stephen Holden in the *New York Times*: "Its shelf life may not be long, nor will it probably be a big hit, since the laughter it provokes is the kind that makes you squirm." The *New York Post*'s Lou Lumenick echoed Holden's sentiment: "*Bamboozled* may not be the year's best movie, but it's undoubtedly the most important." *Salon*'s Andrew O'Hehir had the kindest words of all, finding it to be "a fascinating, enigmatic and, yes, shocking film, a near masterpiece ambiguously balanced between brilliance and incoherence."

More common were negative views, many of which gave off the dual whiffs of indignation and incomprehension. Roger Ebert labeled it "perplexing," warned gravely that "viewers will leave the theater thinking Lee has misused them," and concluded, somewhat presumptuously, that "people's feelings [about blackface] run too strongly and deeply for any satirical use to be effective." Ebert had previously written in 1993 that "the painful history of black-white relations in America is still too sensitive to be joked about crudely," but he was then referring to the bizarre incident in which *Cheers* star Ted Danson—backed by his then-girlfriend Whoopi

Misrepresented People: Bamboozled in Context

Goldberg—appeared at a New York Friars Club celebrity roast wearing blackface, eating watermelon, and telling indefensibly crass jokes. (According to most reports, although everybody knew his name, they weren't so glad he came.)

In the *Chicago Reader*, Jonathan Rosenbaum derided it as "angry ... sloppy, all-over-the-map filmmaking," and mischaracterized Terence Blanchard's mournful, acoustic guitar and piano-led jazz score—an ingeniously gentle counterpoint to the onscreen clamor, and key in providing emotional shading—as "muzak." Armond White, one of the few prominent African American film critics, railed in the *New York Press* that "*Bamboozled* resembles a padded cell with which Hollywood has provided Lee to bounce off walls." He charged Lee with taking valuable screen space from more worthwhile black independent filmmakers like Charles Burnett (*Killer of Sheep*, *To Sleep With Anger*). White also took issue with what he saw as a paradox inherent in Lee's critique of a corporate system within which the director, as a frequent creator of unabashedly commercial product, was deeply enmeshed.

The New Yorker's British critic Anthony Lane, meanwhile, found the whole endeavor quite simply unnecessary for our enlightened age, sniffing that "enough has changed" since the dark days of a blackfaced Al Jolson vamping it up in *The Jazz Singer* (1928), "for audiences to know that blackface is ugly and unfunny." Shortly after

Bamboozled's release, Lane's argument was somewhat undermined by articles from Ted Gioia in *The New York Times* and Robert Moss in *The Los Angeles Times* which attempted to rescue the reputation of Al Jolson, "the king of blackface" [Moss's words], from Lee's contamination.

Like Lane, Andrew Sarris, writing in the *New York Observer*, opted to measure *Bamboozled*'s success by the perceived degree to which it would strike a chord with white liberal sensibilities—in the process ignoring the possibility that it may resonate in some way with black and wider audiences: "It might be argued that Mr. Lee has decided to shock Whitey one last time by rubbing his nose in the blackface obscenities of the past. The problem is that so-called crossover viewers may be hard to find for this terminally angry and turgid guilt trip. Besides, white liberals have probably digested and deplored all the visual stimuli that black historian Donald Bogle has dispensed in his classic treatise *Toms, Coons, Mulattos, Mammies and Bucks*." In short: get over it.

Slate's David Edelstein served up the saltiest take of all. While stopping short of branding the director uppity, he observed that the "chip on [Lee's] shoulder is fast becoming a tumor," and finally wept that Lee's film "makes it so much easier to resign ourselves to our racism." Edelstein also made a staggering factual error, writing that "[t]he joke, a good one, is that liberal whites, initially horrified, come to adore the show." Perhaps he borrowed the same white

Misrepresented People: *Bamboozled* in Context

liberal blinkers sported by Lane and Sarris, because it is made perfectly clear in *Bamboozled*'s studio performance scenes, through Lee's bold and judicious choice of reaction shots, that the audience is made up of many races and ethnicities who offer a believably diverse range of reactions.

Lee's depiction of black viewers enjoying the show, and even eventually wearing blackface themselves, is crucial, because it situates the film within a complex historical context. For example, even though the NAACP successfully campaigned to have *Amos and Andy*—a TV series based on a radio show about two clownish black Harlemites, written by white men—canceled in 1953, the show did enjoy support from black audiences. In their book *Darkest America: Black Minstrelsy from Slavery to Hip-Hop*, Yuval Taylor and Jake Austen argue that, "[e]ditorials and letters in the black press, a great deal of anecdotal evidence, and one scientific poll suggest that not all black Americans shared the NAACP's position (only 18 percent according to Advertest research, as opposed to 80.8 percent supporting the show). Many blacks simply liked seeing blacks on TV and found the show funny." A similar logic could be applied to the cartoonish but seemingly critic-proof films of Tyler Perry today. In *Bamboozled*, Lee takes pains to illustrate that this isn't just a white thing: everyone's involved.[21]

---

21. There are history books which delve into issues surrounding the origins of blackface performance, like Eric Lott's fascinating *Love & Theft*, which contends that minstrelsy, rather than blossoming from

Facing Blackness

* * *

Bamboozled's relentless assertions that there remains something unspeakably rotten at the core of American entertainment, pulsating out into wider society, are precisely what make it so interesting. That, and its jagged, ragged form and content. With its jumpy, torrential style—facilitated in large part by Sam Pollard's bewildering, random-seeming editing—it's as though the film somehow anticipated the furious visual argot of the 24-hour news cycle or was crafted in the style of the short-attention-span internet culture with which so many of us are now sadly all too familiar: 17 Google tabs open, 4 GChat conversations on the go, plus a couple of roiling Twitter arguments for good measure.

Over subsequent re-viewings, I have come to believe that *Bamboozled* is in fact the central work in Lee's canon—the house on fire to which all roads lead. It features some of the rawest and most successful expressions of his enduring obsessions as a filmmaker, including: his investigations into "blackness" as an identity—what does it mean, and who has the authority to claim it?; his playful, pop-artistic use of the frame and soundtrack to convey a multitude of ambiguous

---

hatred, reflected a white working-class attempt at fostering a transracial union through ironic miming, even if this desire rarely, if ever, transcended the realm of "theft," aka the white appropriation of black expressive forms.

Misrepresented People: *Bamboozled* in Context

and contradictory political slogans and messages; and his depictions of conversations between characters as danger zones fraught with potentially fatal misunderstandings.

Notably, *Bamboozled* represents the zenith of Lee's formal experimentation. Throughout his filmmaking career—from the sudden, glorious switch from black-and-white to color in feature debut *She's Gotta Have It* (1986), to his trademark floating dolly shot, and the anamorphic fish-eye-lens effect which warps a significant portion of somber family drama *Crooklyn* (1994) into pure visual abstraction—Lee has displayed a willingness to play with received notions of traditional cinematic grammar in order to disrupt the viewer's expectations.

He has pushed this no further than in *Bamboozled*, which took a cue from the radical work of the Danish Dogme 95 movement to become the first major American studio film to be shot, mostly, on digital video. I say "mostly" because Lee, working with cinematographer Ellen Kuras, shot the New Millennium Minstrel Show performance scenes on Super-16mm film. These primary color-saturated sequences, juxtaposed with the blurry look of the film's main body, resonate as disturbingly lush, underscoring the ease with which the public is seduced by such appalling material. Kuras also commented in documentary *The Making of Bamboozled* that "[w]hen you put blue light on [blackface], it feels like cast-iron … what a great metaphor for this particular feature in the film. People feel locked in the blackface." There's also something mischievously ironic—and fittingly topsy-turvy—about using film stock for material that would, within the fictional universe of the film, be viewed as live television.

Although the decision to go digital seems to have been related more to budget limitations than aesthetic impulse, the end result is apposite to the subject matter. I've already mentioned the unsettling qualities of *Bamboozled*'s juddering editing patterns, but *Reverse Shot*'s Koresky astutely summarizes the rest of the film's stylistic affect: "[R]arely has Lee's aesthetic been so accurately, spiritually wedded to his ideology—the erratic sound mix, the inconsistent lighting, the sense of multiple cameras jostling for screen supremacy (often Kuras set up more than ten cameras within scenes to capture moments when the actors would least expect it; the effect is not flattering to them) all fruitfully aid this tale of woe and compromise."

Besides its technical merits, *Bamboozled* is also, like a vast swathe of Lee's work, a genuine New York story. To label the city a "character" is a timeworn critical cliché, yet *Bamboozled*'s spatially coherent depiction of bustling, commercial midtown Manhattan—as in other media satires like *Network*, Sydney Pollack's *Tootsie* (1982), and Martin Scorsese's *The King of Comedy* (1983)—is central to the viewer's appreciation of the ambient tension brewing between the haves and have-nots, the wannabes and neverwills.

Now, I should be clear at this point that I am not claiming to be *Bamboozled*'s lone defender, boldly crusading where others have feared to tread. It has had its share of eloquent advocates down the years. The journal *Cineaste* published a symposium in a 2001 issue that acknowledged the film's cultural importance, and featured enlightening contributions from, among others, critic Greg Tate, who argued that it posits "minstrelsy as the currency of success in the African American negotiations with white corporate America." In his excellent essay "Bamboozled: In the Mirror of Abjection," film scholar Ed Guerrero lauded it as a film that "takes a tangled problem, the (mis)representation of black people through the generalized performance of neo-minstrelsy, and reworks this performance into a resistant, painfully satirical text that provokes useful debate and critique."

In 2012, culture website *Vulture.com* listed *Bamboozled* as the seventh best film of Lee's career, noting its brave, unyielding fury, and stating that "it's amazing Lee ever got to make another Hollywood movie after this." Todd McGowan, author of the Contemporary Film Directors book series entry on Lee, observed that "its power stems from its unrelenting indictment of our capacity to be duped by racist tropes, especially at the moments when we think we have transcended them," and concluded that "*Bamboozled* is Lee's most disturbing film and his greatest success because it never leaves the terrain of excess—with its intense and constant concern with racist imagery—and yet it creates a sense of everyday reality out of its excesses." In a 2014 column, *The A.V. Club*'s A. A. Dowd got to the heart of one of the more troubling aspects defining much of the negative reaction toward the film: "Lee, so often accused of 'playing the race card,' made a movie that takes aim at the type of folks who use the expression 'playing the race card.' No wonder the film's unpopular."

And yet, it is my belief that *Bamboozled* remains sorely under-appreciated and under-seen. At the time of writing[22], it is out of print on DVD, having only been issued once in 2001 (in an albeit excellent package crammed with special features), is rarely screened on television, and is currently unavailable to stream on any major VOD platforms (Netflix, Amazon Prime, etc.) This is surely an undeserving fate for that rare beast in American cinema: a major studio work which fearlessly explores the corrosive, lasting effects of the racial stereotypes forged in Hollywood's early days and beyond.

---

22. The time of writing was July 2015. In March 2020, *Bamboozled* was finally released on Blu-ray by The Criterion Collection.

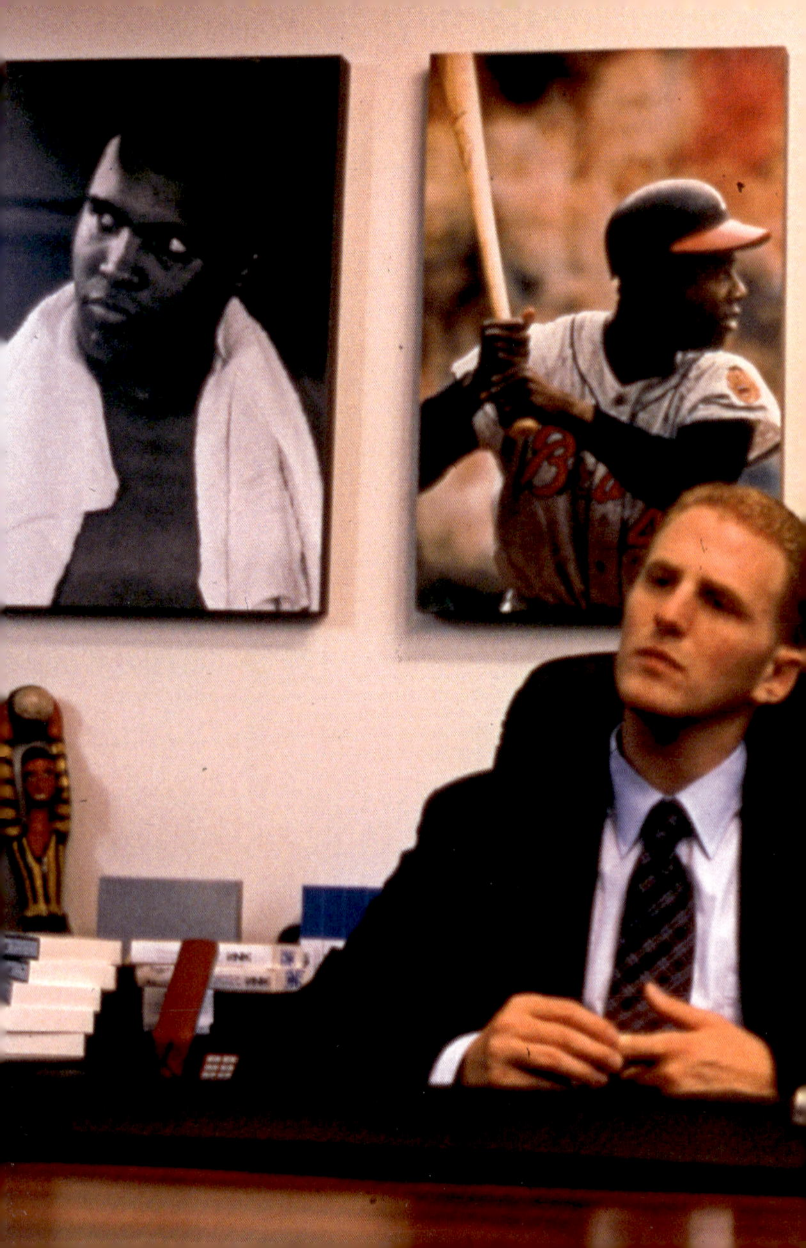

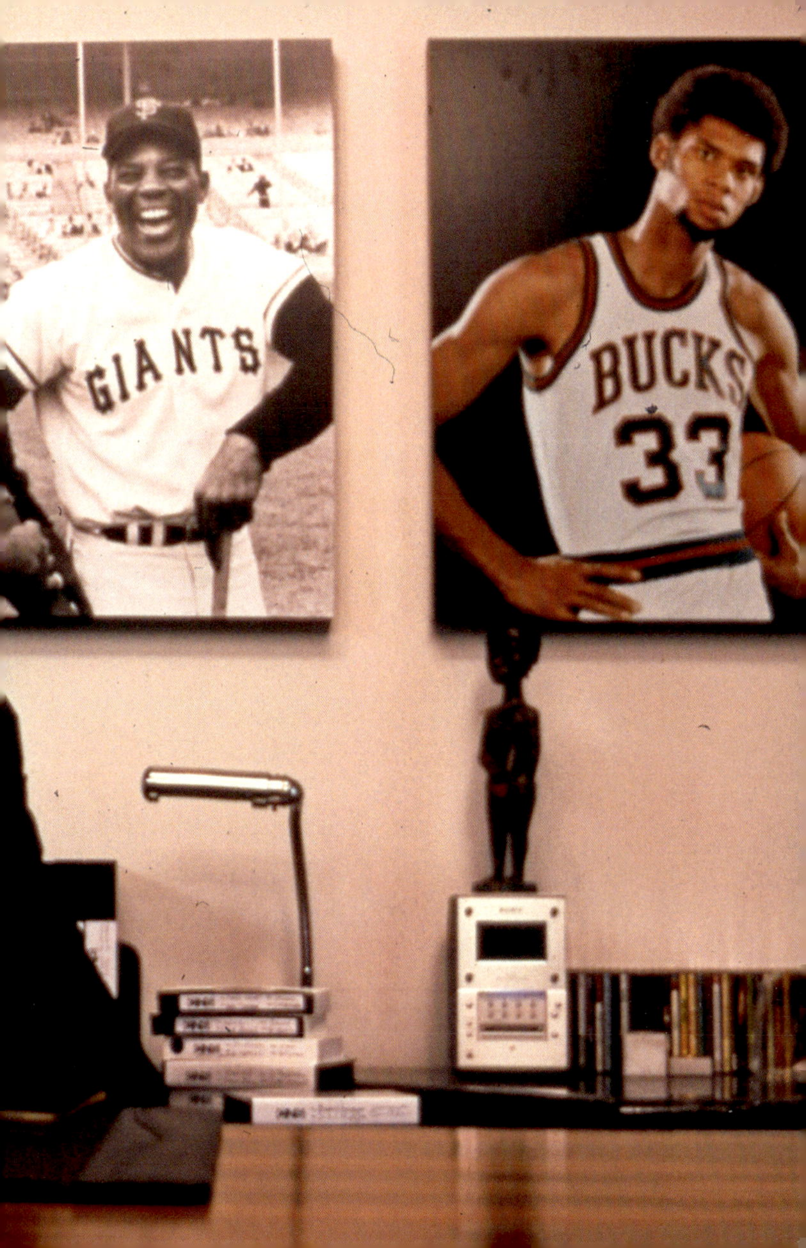
GIANTS
BUCKS
33

Dela Soulless:

Madness, Media, and the Mask

Bamboozled is a maximalist work stuffed with incident, social commentary, and inter-textual media references. Its tone vacillates between starkly dramatic and broadly comedic, frequently in the same scene. How best, then, to get to grips with such a deliberately tricky text?

The place to begin is by closely studying the dubious figure at the heart of the chaos. Part-wrecking ball and part-puppet, Pierre Delacroix pinballs from situation to situation in New York like a buppie incarnation of Ralph Ellison's *Invisible Man*, considering himself—almost always wrongly—to be ahead of the game. Though unlike that classic narrator in African American literature, Delacroix winds up a hopeless case, on his way to the grave rather than plotting a brighter future for himself. How *does* this all transpire? The answers are complex but, as we will see, their roots lie in a vicious, intractable bend of personal failings, historical ghosts, and institutional malaise.

However, interesting things are happening even before we are formally introduced to our protagonist. *Bamboozled*'s first image is a high-angle shot of a giant transparent clock face, which doubles as a large window in a lavish loft apartment in Brooklyn's Dumbo district. The steely blue hue of the image, in tandem with the shockingly fuzzy digital picture quality, makes the cars outside look as though they are driving underwater. The camera spirals slowly down from its queasy height to find a man in silk pajamas splayed out on luxury purple sheets. He is wide-awake and looks perturbed, his fingers and toes flexing agitatedly to an unknowable rhythm. A sudden cut to a wide shot from the opposite end of the room reveals that the clock is positioned directly above where he sleeps. Time, you might say, hangs heavy on his head, and it could well be running out.

The man subsequently goes about his morning routines, like brushing his teeth and shaving his head in the mirror—the first of many reflected images Lee will deploy in this tale of fractured identity. Lee then throws a curveball: A voiceover, delivered in a plummy, stilted tone, proceeds to outline the Webster dictionary definition of satire, as follows:

1. (a) A literary work in which human vice or folly is ridiculed or attacked scornfully

1. (b) The branch of literature which composes such work

2. Irony, derision or caustic wit used to attack, expose folly, vice or stupidity

In his DVD commentary, Lee states that the inclusion of this definition is meant to make utterly unambiguous the film's intentions—it allows its excesses to unfold through a satirical filter; what you are about to see is not supposed to be "real life." But it's difficult to see *Bamboozled* in a classical satirical sense, in which the viewer can openly identify with the work's author (Lee) by joining in a sustained attack on one single, more powerful target.

Dela Soulless: Madness, Media, and the Mask

(To borrow language from a debate which erupted in the aftermath of the January 2015 terror attacks on French satirical magazine *Charlie Hebdo*, *Bamboozled* doesn't "punch up," or "punch down"; rather it clenches its fists and runs windmiling down the street.) When the dust settles on this tale of poor taste and thwarted ambition, one might also be inclined to consider *Bamboozled* as falling more in line with critic Northrup Frye's definition of Menippean satire, which, as cited by Stuart Klawans in *The Nation*: "[d]eals less with people as such than with mental attitudes. Pedants, bigots, cranks, parvenus, virtuosi, enthusiasts, rapacious and incompetent professional men of all kinds, are handled in terms of their occupational approach to life as distinct from their social behavior."

During the man's speech, the old-timey instrumental backing of Stevie Wonder's aforementioned song "Misrepresented People"—which plays high in the mix—gives way to a thumping contemporary hip-hop beat. This upsurge in energy is complemented by a sudden cut to a tight shot of the face and chest of the man. He's now nattily dressed in rimless spectacles, three shades of purple, and is staring directly into the camera at the viewer. He's also sporting a curious smile that curls upward beneath his Kid Creole pencil mustache. His mood now, oddly, seems to contradict his apparent unease when we first see him. As he begins speaking, it quickly becomes clear that it is he who delivered the voiceover.

"Bonjour! My name is Pierre *De-la-croix*," he announces, torturing those final syllables into a preposterous mishmash of French and British accents. In the ensuing monologue, he outlines his position as a writer at a company whose ratings are failing due to the onslaught of multi-channel options, video, the internet, and interactive gaming. ("I am one of those people responsible for what *you* view on your idiot box … you're like rats, fleeing a sinking ship!" he admonishes contemptuously.) While he speaks, his long fingers—the left fourth and right pinkie adorned with flashy gold rings—continually enter and exit the frame as they clench and curl, occasionally extending to point straight ahead; it's like they have a life of their own. On first impressions, this is one creepy guy.

As the viewer concentrates on Delacroix's words (and fingers), they will also notice that the background moves behind him while his head remains perfectly still: it's as though he's traveling around his apartment on a Segway machine, or simply hovering in midair. Those familiar with Lee's work will recognize this as the director's signature shot, in which he sets up a dolly as per usual, then puts the actor on another dolly, and moves the camera and the actor at the same time, creating a discomfiting floating effect. Although this use of the shot has none of the transcendental emotional clout of its greatest iteration, in *Malcolm X* (when Malcolm is in a daze, heading toward the place of his eventual assassination), it's nonetheless bold of Lee to bring his big trick out of the cupboard so quickly. The device's distancing effect works in tandem with Delacroix's startling theatrics to create an experience entirely in opposition to conventional notions of seamlessly immersing the viewer into a film's world.

Within little more than a single minute of screen time, *Bamboozled* bombards the viewer with a catalog of deliberate formal and authorial dissonance, brilliantly foreshadowing its forthcoming protean style. We get the stentorian, impossible-to-ignore invocations of Wonder on the soundtrack competing with the unmistakable directorial stamp of Lee, and the spooky division of Delacroix's presence into three separate forms: alive as a subjective character in the present tense; as an interlocutor with direct access to the viewer through the camera lens; and possibly speaking from beyond the grave in voiceover. (Another canny direct reference: to William Holden's character Joe Gillis in *Sunset Boulevard* [1950]—although Gillis's eventual dead-or-alive status is less ambiguous: he starts the film floating face down in a swimming pool.)

Pierre Delacroix is portrayed by Damon Wayans, a versatile comic actor who, after small roles in films including *Beverly Hills Cop* (1984), came to major prominence on the Emmy award-winning sketch show *In Living Color*, which ran on the Fox network from 1990-94, and was notable for featuring a predominantly African American cast. From his extravagant dress to his bourgeois affectations and demeanor, Delacroix is the strangest character to appear in Lee's entire filmographic rogue's gallery of weirdos, agitators, vagabonds, fall-guys and criminals—and that's saying something. (Ritchie, the pretend Cockney punk-slash-sex worker played by Adrien Brody in the overheated *Summer of Sam* [1999], may feel aggrieved at missing out on this title.)

Wayans explained the genesis of his approach to the role in a hilarious anecdote in *The Making of Bamboozled*:

> "A week before I came to New York to work on this I met a man called Danville. He was a writer, but he was a waiter first. He had to wait until he wrote. The guy was so full of contradictions. He would say 'I don't respect anyone. There are only two writers living that I respect. One is … I don't know … and the other … the names have escaped me right now, but they are brilliant.' He didn't know either of their names! I said, 'I gotta do him!'"

Wayans brings this absurd blend of cluelessness and arrogance to an individual who, argues *Salon*'s Michael Sragow, "seems to have stylized himself into a parody of white cultivation," most likely as an attempted means of advancement in a white, corporate world in which African Americans largely lack the institutional presence and power to represent themselves in a consistently multifaceted way. I think that Sragow is partially correct in his judgment—it's hard not to see a stereotyped "white" affectation in the character; Delacroix's real name, we later discover,

Dela Soulless: Madness, Media, and the Mask

is Peerless Dothan, and he has substituted this bestowed signifier of uplift and confidence, which likely has its roots in the black church, for a made-up self-brand befitting an 18th century French sophisticate, but which still bears religious undertones ("Delacroix" translates as "Of the cross"). I suspect his new name may also be an oblique echo of W. E. B. DuBois, the influential African American scholar and famed "New Negro"[23] who argued that it was the responsibility of a "talented tenth" of black elites and intellectuals to uplift the race (Delacroix is fond of referring to himself as a "Negro").

And yet, as we will see, flashes of Delacroix's ingrained, intractable black identity emerge when he is confronted by the most insidious forms of institutional racism. His callous betrayal of fellow African Americans—street performers Manray and Womack—stems from his inability to effectively process the corrosive pain of being disrespected as a black man himself.

Many critics at the time of the film's original release found Wayans' devoutly non-naturalistic performance difficult to take seriously, and thus dismissed it as an overblown caricature. I would contend that the actor, with impressive poise and technical control, successfully

---

23. "New Negro" is a term popularized during the Harlem Renaissance implying a more outspoken advocacy of dignity, and a refusal to submit quietly to the practices and laws of Jim Crow racial segregation. It was made popular by the writer Alain LeRoy Locke.

conveys the sense that Delacroix has become so engaged in his heightened, high-wire act of identity that he no longer knows, deep down, who he is, or ever really was. He wears a permanent mask, the rigorous maintenance of which is the cornerstone of a genuinely unsettling, if often amusing, performance.

Delacroix is certainly odd enough to feel *sui generis*, but he's not alone in the filmography of Lee, who has featured dubious "white-acting" characters in his work. The most obvious is the conk-haired, finicky über-buppie Greer Childs (John Canada Terrell) from *She's Gotta Have It* (1986), who petulantly cuts ties with his paramour Nola (Tracy Camilla Johns) by announcing: "You never had any drive or ambition. I'm gonna go up to Manhattan to get me a white girl." Greer reeks of unfettered aspiration, and Lee deliberately aligns his wannabe "whiteness" with unpleasantness, particularly when contrasted against Lee's own character, the lovably goofy bike messenger Mars Blackmon, or Nola's third love interest, the earthy, down-home Brooklyn boy Jamie Overstreet (Tommy Hicks). Then there's the comic-odious Wendell (the incomparable Wendell Pierce) in the underrated *Get on the Bus* (1996). Wendell is a brash Republican car salesman who joins a large group of African American men on a bus bound for the Million Man March in Washington D.C. This diverse bunch spend much of the film bickering over personal issues and politics, and it's only the appearance of this individualistic scoundrel who unites them. They eventually collaborate to hurl him from the bus in much the same way that Uncle Phil would routinely dispatch Jazz (DJ Jazzy Jeff) through the front door of his mansion in *The Fresh Prince of Bel-Air*.

Delacroix is also part of a broader lineage of historical and artistic conversations about what constitutes "blackness," and specifically the existential complexity informing the experiences of black people operating in majority white spaces.

One literary ancestor of Delacroix is Max Disher, the protagonist of George S. Schuyler's astonishing satirical science fiction novel *Black No More* (1931). Disher believes that, as an ambitious young black man in 1930s New York, there are three options to succeed: "Get out, get white, or get along." So, he takes advantage of a new skin bleaching technology, pioneered by one Dr. Junius Crookman, to "get white," with ultimately disastrous consequences. Like *Bamboozled*, *Black No More* does not restrict itself to one line of satirical inquiry. Instead, while exposing "race" itself as a deeply problematic social construct, it takes aim at myriad targets, including: its protagonist's self-absorption; the multilayered evils of white supremacy; and prominent leaders of both the NAACP and the Harlem Renaissance.

Leaping forward, I see shades of Delacroix's crisis in the eponymous, real-life protagonist of Wendell B. Harris's stunning Sundance-winner *Chameleon Street* (1989):

William Douglas Street is a successful career conman, played with great cunning by Harris, whose mind gradually disintegrates as he worms his way into the upper echelons of white professional society. A similar theme drives Michael Schultz's perceptive, underrated comedy *Livin' Large* (1991), about an aspiring black TV anchorman named Dexter Jackson (the excellent Terrence C. Carson) who wonders whether becoming successful also means "selling out." As he climbs higher in the corporate structure, and leaves his working class roots behind, he is visited by increasingly horrifying visions of his whiteface alter ego.

Lee has explored the travails of lone black figures in white corporate spaces in his own work: from *Jungle Fever* (1991), in which successful architect Flipper Purify (Wesley Snipes) is prevented by his oily white bosses from attaining partner status; to *She Hate Me* (2004), whose protagonist Jack Armstrong (Anthony Mackie), an upwardly mobile biotech exec, is falsely accused of fraud by his corrupt bigwig boss (Woody Harrelson). Lee casts Armstrong as a proud, ethical hero[24] in a sordid world of establishment corruption, and parallels his story with that of the real-life black security guard Frank Willis (played in flashback by Chiwetel Ejiofor) who blew the whistle

---

24. Jack Armstrong also spends a great deal of the film impregnating lesbians for money, but trying to adequately parse the stunningly overstuffed *She Hate Me* would take a great deal more space than I have available to me here.

Dela Soulless: Madness, Media, and the Mask

on the Watergate break-in, yet struggled with joblessness before dying at 52. These men are not motivated by a desire to ape white society; rather they wish to be respected and recognized as individuals. Flipper and Jack emerge with considerably more dignity and integrity than Delacroix, suggesting that while institutional racism is an ongoing and widespread problem in Lee's vision of America, he views the media industry—of which he has plenty of first-hand experience—as particularly corrosive on the spirit.

Delacroix is also in some ways reminiscent of the eponymous figure in Robert Downey Sr.'s madcap drama *Putney Swope* (1969): a token black on the executive board of an advertising firm who is accidentally placed in charge. But Swope has radical, rather than self-absorbed and satirical plans: he renames the business "Truth and Soul, Inc.," and replaces the white staff with his black militant brothers.

However, the most obvious precursor to Delacroix is the character of Bruford Jamison (Eriq LaSalle) in Clark Johnson's bombastic satire *Drop Squad* (1994), on which Lee served as executive producer. *Drop Squad* follows a group of violent black neo-revolutionaries—significant traces of whose flailing venom can be detected in *Bamboozled*'s Mau Maus—who kidnap and "de-program," via mental and physical torture, individuals they consider Uncle Toms, a term used to connote a black person who is perceived to have internalized "white" values and/or acts against the interests of other black people. Clarence Thomas, the controversial Supreme Court judge who, in 2013, compared affirmative action to slavery, is only one notable example of a public figure who has been widely labeled with the derogatory term. In *Bamboozled*, Delacroix is explicitly compared to Thomas on local radio.

Bruford becomes one of the Squad's targets, thanks to his collusion in the misrepresentation of African Americans by conceptualizing campaigns for products that are cynically targeted at low-income black consumers. In this overcooked film's best scene (which for once strikes the optimum combination of screamingly funny and hideously bleak) Lee cameos as a hungry customer in a commercial for 'Gospel Pak', a brand of Evangelical Christian-themed fried chicken that's served with a verse of scripture printed on each napkin. As we will discover, Lee borrowed the concept of the fake commercial for *Bamboozled* with brutal satirical effect.

Bruford shows hints of compunction and self-awareness, and has a group of buppie pals to bounce off—some of them are considerably more unpleasant than him. Yet Delacroix, save for his assistant Sloan, is a loner: his outsider status is made abundantly clear when we first see him striding through the corridors of CNS HQ, proffering forced, rictus "hellos" to a string of white colleagues. It's only when we meet his boss, Dunwitty (Michael Rapaport), that we discover what Delacroix is really up against.

In a film full of vividly drawn performances, Rapaport gives one of the best: he conveys his character's bone-

Dela Soulless: Madness, Media, and the Mask

deep venality with a gleeful, puppyish buoyancy. It makes him dangerously affable, if never quite likable. (When Delacroix later proposes *The New Millennium Minstrel Show*, Dunwitty excitedly squeals "I'm gettin' a boner! Swanson Johnson is gettin' hard!"—his vulgarity is genuinely amusing.) If Delacroix can be accused of acting "white," then Dunwitty is his less ambiguous inverse—the untrammeled white fetishization of black culture made flesh: Elvis Presley, Norman Mailer's "White Negro," and Vanilla Ice rolled into one bumptious, signifyin', ginger-headed package.[25]

One of *Bamboozled*'s most consistently impressive features is its sharp depiction of racial dynamics in the corporate workplace. Lee's portrayal of the relationship between Delacroix and Dunwitty is particularly insightful. In their first meeting, Dunwitty leverages his so-called expertise of "black culture"—no doubt inspired by years of omnivorous consumption—to jovially yet passive-

---

25. Dunwitty represents the 'wigger' archetype at his most obvious and off-putting. In his book *Everything But The Burden*, however, Greg Tate convincingly argues that the "'wigger''s more sophisticated brethren have spent most of the last century trying to translate their Black/white baggage into Western culture's spiritual malaise. In popular music since the sixties, complicated characters like Bob Dylan, Frank Zappa, Joni Mitchell, Steely Dan, Johnny Rotten, (and now Eminem) complicated the question of how race mythology can be convincingly exploited. These are white artists who found ways to express the complexity of American whiteness inside Black musical forms."

aggressively quiz Delacroix on his knowledge of "colored people time," a stereotyped concept which holds that black people have an inherently poor sense of timekeeping. (Delacroix has been mysteriously late for a meeting he claims he didn't know was happening; his assistant, Sloan, maintains that she didn't know about it either. A sly undermining of his character? We never find out.) Delacroix wearily responds with a full explanation—he is, of course, well aware of the cliché.

They begin talking business, and Dunwitty makes his claim to black cultural ownership shockingly clear by blithely declaring: "I probably know niggers better than you. I don't give a damn what that prick Spike Lee says." It's a bracingly funny, significant line. Firstly, it shows that Dunwitty feels entitled to use a word that has a complex history: most notably it's been deployed, by white people, as the most extreme epithet with which to insult and dehumanize black people. Of course, black people—including countless comedians and musicians—have historically sought to reclaim the word in order to defuse its power and imbue it with new meanings. Comic Dick Gregory even titled his 1964 autobiography *Nigger*, and appeared in Horace Ové's fascinating documentary *Baldwin's Nigger* (1969), in which he and the author James Baldwin addressed a predominantly Afro-Caribbean audience in London on the subject of the social situation for black people in Britain and the United States.

Dela Soulless: Madness, Media, and the Mask

It's likely that, in Dunwitty's mind, he's using the safely "reclaimed" version of the word—whether "nigger" or its derivative "nigga"—and he seems perfectly earnest in his belief that it isn't the slightest bit problematic. (Many white media figures—from Madonna to Tom Hanks's risible rapper son Chet Haze[26]—have come under fire for the same offense; Lee isn't making this stuff up.) In practice, Dunwitty's use of the term exemplifies appropriation at its most insidious: he's eliding the complicity of white people in its hateful history in order to shamelessly perform blackness-as-coolness *in front* of a black person. ("Brotherman, I'm blacker than you!" he tells Delacroix.) Aside from summoning up the ghosts of blackface minstrelsy, in which white performers would wear blackface and communicate a perverse yet supposedly "authentic" vision of blackness, it leaves Delacroix in an invidious position. Because Dunwitty holds executive institutional power and privilege in the exchange, Delacroix is helpless to curb the offense or, one suspects, prevent it from further metastasizing through the culture of the corporation and out into the public domain.

---

26. As Gawker tartly reported in June 2015: "Chester 'Chet Haze' Hanks, caucasian son of beloved caucasian Hollywood A-lister Tom Hanks, took to Instagram this weekend to vociferously share his feelings on Hating Ass Niggaz." The next day Haze offered a classic nonapology: "Some people will get it, some people won't. Either way, Ima keep living my life however the fuck I want. ALL LOVE."

Delacroix politely requests that Dunwitty refrain from using the term, to no avail. Then, in a brief daydream-sequence, connoted by a blurry, in-camera effect, the type of which you might see in a home-made horror film, Delacroix imagines himself furiously boxing Dunwitty about the ears. This subjective switch of perspective confirms Delacroix's burgeoning black pride and anger—but its realization is only a fantasy: internalized and inwardly corrosive.

Meanwhile, by including his own name in the script, Lee plays the role of pop provocateur—it's a brazen breakage of the fourth wall to humorously, if also somewhat sourly, acknowledge his outspoken public persona, and reference his part in a volatile real-life debate. In 1997, Lee publicly criticized Quentin Tarantino for his frequent use of the word "nigger" in his scripts[27]: "Quentin is infatuated with

---

27. Its most egregious manifestation occurs in *Pulp Fiction* (1994), in which Tarantino cast himself as Jimmy, a deadbeat schmo with a black wife—a wordless, briefly-glimpsed fantasy figure. Jimmy is visited by hitmen Jules (Samuel L. Jackson) and Vincent (John Travolta), who've brought a present: the dead body of Marvin (Phil Lamarr), a young black man whose head has been graphically splattered by a stray bullet from Vincent's gun. Jimmy takes this opportunity to repeatedly and sarcastically ask the men if they see "a sign in my house that says 'dead nigger storage?'" The scene is equal parts cringeworthy and offensive and, crucially—unlike in *Bamboozled*—the epithet's frequent usage has no discernible critical or contextual edge. Instead, it's deployed merely as a glib signifier of one tool's cool. Every time it arrives when I'm watching *Pulp Fiction*—a film I generally enjoy—I'm jolted out of the experience. The combination of the fetishization of black death, black

Dela Soulless: Madness, Media, and the Mask

that word," he told *Variety*. "What does he want to be made—an honorary black man?"[28]

The meeting between Dunwitty and Delacroix ends on a pointed note. After the former has unceremoniously quashed the latter's dreams of creating a show targeted at middle-class black audiences, he gestures to a portrait hanging on the wall offscreen. Like a gangsta rapper flashing his cash, he offers Delacroix a thousand dollars if he can identify the sportsman depicted. Delacroix, of course, hasn't the foggiest idea who it is, and has thus "failed" in this entirely superficial game to "prove" his blackness. In later scenes, we see the full scale of Dunwitty's interior decor, featuring African masks and prominently displayed prints, taken by photographer Neil Leifert, of black sports stars like Mike Tyson and Muhammad Ali. This imagery offers a fascinating ideological complement to the claim made by hot-tempered politico Buggin' Out (Giancarlo Esposito) in *Do The Right Thing* that the local Italian-American pizza place needs "some brothers up on

---

women and Quentin Tarantino's acting (he gives an absolutely dreadful performance) is too much to handle. Dunwitty, too, has a black wife and biracial children: he might as well be Jimmy in disguise.

28. In a further ironic twist, Tarantino actually appeared—in a self-satirizing role—in Lee's *Girl 6* (1996), as a sleazy director who makes a black actress strip in an audition; his character claims an expert, territorial knowledge of black actresses and how black womanhood should be represented on film.

the wall," because a mostly black clientele spends their money there, and thus deserves representation. Well, there are nothing *but* "brothers on the wall" in Dunwitty's office.

Taken at face value, these are images of black excellence being celebrated in an artistic way. Perhaps they are, on one level, exemplifiers of Lee's own taste—fans of *Do The Right Thing* will recall that, in one memorable shot, he lingers on a giant wall mural of Mike Tyson to underline his status as a hero for the local Bed-Stuy community, while Lee also made a fortune directing numerous iconic commercials for Nike starring Michael Jordan in the 80s and 90s. And yet, in this specific context the pictures represent the commodification of blackness as combative and athletic; they are looming signifiers that, in the imagination of people like Dunwitty, black people exist primarily as sports stars and entertainers.[29]

This echoes yet another exchange in *Do The Right Thing* between pizza deliveryman Mookie (Lee) and his hardcore racist colleague Pino (John Turturro), when the former challenges the latter to explain why, if he is so virulently anti-black, his favorite singer is Prince, his favorite sportsman is Magic Johnson, and his favorite actor

---

29. Does Lee have a part to play in this widespread lionization of sports stars? Arguably yes, but then he's also spent most of his career creating a raft of diverse and substantial roles for black and Latino actors, in the process helping to launch the careers of Samuel L. Jackson, Laurence Fishburne, Rosie Perez and Wesley Snipes, among many others.

is Eddie Murphy? "They're not niggers… they're *more* than black," comes Pino's weak reply. Pino, though, is a pizza boy, not a media gatekeeper with vast influence in shaping the cultural conversation.

The result of this crucial, beautifully-observed establishing scene is to underscore the impossibility of Delacroix's position within the corporate structure, capsulize his simmering frustration, and convey the tinderbox of unequal power relations from which the forthcoming madness will erupt.[30]

* * *

The merciless lampooning of corporate media cluelessness is *Bamboozled*'s most consistently effective line of satirical attack. Early in the film, Dunwitty casually mentions that if he experiences any blowback from activists, he'll simply pay off the NAACP ("I've dealt with those guys before"). His arrogance may seem over the top, but one only needs to look at the emails between Sony executives Scott Rudin and Amy Pascal, which leaked in December 2014, to see that

---

30. One further stranger-than-fiction convolution: Lee and Rapaport publicly clashed in 2014 over the subject of gentrification in New York—an issue in which race, class, and finance are endemic factors. Lee called Rapaport "stupid," and said he "doesn't know what he's fucking talking about." Rapaport called Lee a "shit stain." Rapaport's real-life demeanor, for the record, isn't a million miles away from that of Dunwitty.

comparable brackishness can flourish at the very top level of cultural gatekeeping: these emails included a string of tasteless jokes, along crassly racial lines, about the supposed film taste of President Barack Obama.

There's a sharply-drawn scene in which a self-satisfied Delacroix, flying high after Dunwitty's initial endorsement of his idea, addresses a room of staff writers, the make-up of which is overwhelmingly white. There are no black faces to be seen, save for he and Sloan. This evidently well-meaning but hopelessly naive group deflect Delacroix's concerns about diversity with depressingly predictable replies: "It would be better to have some African American writers, but for whatever reason, they're not here"; "…maybe they couldn't find any people with experience, or they wouldn't work for the pay, or refused to work on the show."

Lee punctuates the scene with lightning bolt-like cuts to clips from catchphrase-heavy 70s and 80s TV shows (Sherman Hemsley in *The Jeffersons*, Pigmeat Markham in *Laugh-In*) to underscore the writers' shockingly open admissions that, despite their responsibility for crafting representations of black life for mainstream audiences, their knowledge of actual black life is almost entirely limited to broad televisual depictions. Delacroix also broaches the real-life murder trial of O. J. Simpson to coax out some of the group's deeper prejudices—another sharp comment from Lee on how media narratives intersect with, and influence, personal and political beliefs.

Dela Soulless: Madness, Media, and the Mask

Later, Delacroix's patience runs out entirely with Myrna Goldfarb, the white Jewish media consultant hired by Dunwitty to pre-emptively smooth over any controversy. When she announces that she has a PhD from Yale in African American studies, Delacroix responds with a viciously funny—and cruel—ad hominem attack: "So, you fucked a Negro in college? Continue, o great niggerologist!" This sequence particularly upset *Slate* critic David Edelstein, who wrote that "Sloan and De-La don't buy her empathy, and neither does the movie. I'd like to say that any Jews who'd appear in a Spike Lee 'joint' are traitors to their people, but I'm afraid I'd sound too much like Lee."[31] I'd contend that this scene, while necessarily prickly and uncomfortable, mercilessly exposes a paternalistic attitude inherent in certain strands of white liberalism, which James Baldwin summarized thusly in 1965: "I have one thing against White Liberals which is their assumption that their morality and what they take to be civilization and their religion is something which I need. What I resent is

---

31. Lee has faced criticism in some quarters for his use of stereotypes, particularly black women; Jewish characters like Goldfarb and business owners Mo and Jo Flatbush in *Mo' Better Blues* (1990); and working class Italian-Americans in *Jungle Fever* and *Summer of Sam*. I think Todd McGowan makes a good argument when he writes "There are points at which Lee slips into blatant stereotyping, but his films run this risk because they themselves operate in the same manner as stereotypes do—by focusing on excess. The difference is that stereotypes simply display and use excess, while Lee explores its use in his films."

the assumption that I must be raised to their level." Almost as if describing Goldfarb, he also wrote that "[a] liberal is someone who thinks he knows more about your experience than you do." One can sense the righteous anger rising in Delacroix when he exclaims to Goldfarb, "These are Negroes we're talking about. Not some lab mice in a cage. We are not one monolithic group of people. We do not all think, look, and act alike!"

Goldfarb may be a broadly-drawn caricature, but her attitude, like that of Dunwitty, is rooted in an authentic strain of ostensibly liberal thought which falls ambiguously between extreme respect and sociopathy. On this subject, we may consider the bizarre case of Rachel Dolezal, the president of the Spokane, Washington chapter of the NAACP, whose parents came forward in June 2015 to announce that their daughter was in fact white, and had been posing as black for a number of years, faux-fro and all: "This is not some freak, *Birth of a Nation*, mockery blackface performance," Dolezal told Matt Lauer in a TV interview. She may have meant well, and worked in service of African American rights, but she had the luxury of being able to abandon her "blackness" at any moment—a fact which calls to mind the witty title of Greg Tate's book of essays on the issue of white appropriation of black culture: *Everything But The Burden*.

In a different film, the presence of outsize characters like Dunwitty and Goldfarb might be derailing. But Lee

Dela Soulless: Madness, Media, and the Mask

brilliantly neutralizes this potential issue by integrating real-world, larger-than-life figures into the text, from flamboyant civil rights activist Al Sharpton, to celebrity lawyer Johnny Cochran, who are both briefly and entirely plausibly depicted picketing the show outside CNS towers. At the height of the show's national popularity, Lee even takes us briefly inside the White House, where we find then-President Bill Clinton watching along (it's genuine archive footage, with the fictional show digitally transposed onto the television). He claps his hands like a seal and announces, in his trademark southern drawl, "I *like* this!" Is Lee making an oblique reference to the controversial comment made in 1998 by the African American Nobel laureate Toni Morrison that Clinton, "white skin notwithstanding… is our first black President … [he] displays almost every trope of blackness: single-parent household, born poor, working-class, saxophone-playing, McDonald's-and-junk-food-loving boy from Arkansas?" The crux of Morrison's argument was that, since the Whitewater real estate scandal of 1992, Bill Clinton had been mistreated by the media because of his "blackness," the tropes of which Morrison outlined in her article. Like much of *Bamboozled*, the sequence is resistant to a concrete interpretation, but even this throwaway moment is rich in tantalizing, meta-media commentary.

* * *

Sometimes, though, *Bamboozled*'s satire is downright muddy. Given that authorial control of the pilot episode of *Mantan: The New Millennium Minstrel Show* is ultimately taken away from Delacroix, and we're never clued into the specifics of its creation, the aim of its incendiary content is opaque. Perhaps this is a riff, from Lee, on the bureaucracy of network television writing: when the process is so messy, how can the finished product exhibit clarity of vision, or its content be accurately accounted for?

Whatever the case, Mantan's *Network*-referencing speech is fascinating. "I'm tired of the drugs, I'm tired of the crack babies born out of wedlock to crackhead, AIDS-infested parents ... I want you to go to your windows," he hollers, "Yell out, scream with all the life you can muster up inside your bruised, battered, assaulted bodies, 'I'm sick and tired of niggers and I'm not gonna take it anymore!'"

This invective seems to be directly inspired by an infamous 1996 routine delivered by comedian Chris Rock, in which he outlined the differences between "black men" and "niggas"—the latter referring to the criminals and layabouts supposedly bringing down the reputation of the race. An under-fire Rock retired the routine because, as he said in a 2005 interview with *60 Minutes*, "some people that were racist thought they had license to say nigger."

Even so, the routine became an influential reference point in a burgeoning school of thought often dubbed "respectability politics," which blamed a nebulous pathology,

Dela Soulless: Madness, Media, and the Mask

rather than the lingering effects of slavery, historical discrimination, and structural racism, for problems within black communities. Some of the most notable exegeses of this ideology appeared in John McWhorter's 2000 book *Losing the Race: Self-Sabotage in Black America*; the 2004 "Pound Cake" speech by the now-disgraced Bill Cosby ("Looking at the incarcerated, these are not political criminals ... People getting shot in the back of the head over a piece of pound cake!"); and the jaw-dropping 2006 *Esquire* article "The Manifesto of Ascendancy for the Modern American Nigger," by future *12 Years a Slave* screenwriter John Ridley. Here's a charming excerpt:

> LET ME TELL YOU SOMETHING ABOUT NIGGERS, the oppressed minority within our minority. Always down. Always out. Always complaining that they can't catch a break. Notoriously poor about doing for themselves. Constantly in need of a leader but unable to follow in any direction that's navigated by hard work, self-reliance. And though they spliff and drink and procreate their way onto welfare doles and WIC lines, niggers will tell you their state of being is no fault of their own. They are not responsible for their nearly 5 percent incarceration rate and their 9.2 percent unemployment rate. Not responsible for the 11.8 percent rate at which they drop out of high school. For the 69.3 percent of births they create out of wedlock.

The difference between this grisly text and Mantan's rant—whoever wrote it—is barely discernible. Delacroix partially echoes its rhetoric when he appears on DJ Imhotep

Gary Byrd's radio show to unconvincingly defend *Mantan*: "Slavery has been over 400 years ago," he splutters, incorrectly. "We need to stop thinking about the white man this, the white man that, this is the new millennium!" But it's obvious by this point that Delacroix is floundering: he is the public face of a runaway phenomenon he partially created, but cannot fully comprehend.

The film also has a remarkably sour streak, particularly in its unsparing treatment of the Mau Maus, who, after having been rejected by *The New Millennium Minstrel Show* at audition stage, become furious at its stereotyped depictions of black people.

Lee aims to communicate the irony that the Mau Maus are in fact guilty of this crime themselves: they are a naive, volatile rabble with low intellect, destructive tendencies, and a fondness for chugging Hennessy cognac and "Da Bomb" malt liquor (which happens to be one of *Mantan*'s main sponsors, as we discover in a riotously funny faux-commercial starring Honeycutt: its alcohol content is so high it makes him breathe fire.) Their conversations frequently descend into meaningless babble—"Know what I mean, know what I'm saying?" they repeat to each other in one scene, without making a single cogent point. Yet despite their largely cretinous nature, they also understand the power of mass media. When they decide to act on their anger, their leader, Big Blak Afrika, announces that it needs to be "some global blowout shit; this gotta have some symbolism and iconography—this gotta be like John Carlos and Tommie Smith" —at which point Lee cuts to the famed image of the 1968 Olympians with their fists raised in the iconic Black Power salute.

The Mau Maus never quite add up, though. Lee is unable to convincingly square their supposed idiocy with their bubbling, pan-African political consciousness and conviction. It's jarringly implausible, even in a self-described satire, that they would reference the anti-colonial thinker Frantz Fanon, argue for slavery reparations, *and* desire a slice of the corporate pie (unless their argument—never effectively articulated in Lee's screenplay—is that they'd attempt to smash the system from within). Meanwhile Big Blak, as portrayed by real-life rapper Mos Def, is far too personable, laidback and palpably intelligent to pass for a hair-trigger moron: his first conversation with Sloan, a brother-sister back-and-forth rich in button-pushing barbs, subtle wit, and references to Malcolm X's legendary "Message to the Grass Roots" speech, is one of the film's smartest scenes.

Lee would have been on safer ground had he constructed the Mau Maus as a more straightforward parody of materialistic, misogynistic 90s gangsta rap—a genre which he explicitly compared, in interviews, to a 21st century minstrel show. ("I'm not a fan … I think it's obsessed with the 'bling bling' … the titties and the butts shaking and jiggling into the camera. I don't think that's uplifting," he told *Cineaste*.) Lee instead makes a weird, perhaps unintentional mockery of progressive, socially conscious black music and politics, an end result made even odder by the presence of The Roots, a real-life, politically-engaged outfit, who portray the *Mantan* backing band, and the inclusion of Public Enemy's squalling anti-stereotype anthem "Burn Hollywood Burn," which plays on the soundtrack as the Mau Maus are eventually extinguished by the cops.

My guess is that Lee uses the Mau Maus to take a coded potshot at the likes of Amiri Baraka, the radical black playwright and activist who, during the production of *Malcolm X*, mocked Lee in the media as a middle-class buppie, then, having obtained a leaked script of the film, appeared alongside 30 vociferous protestors at a preview screening. In Lee's solitary position as, essentially, the bulwark of black American commercial cinema across some three decades, he's taken flak from all sides: it's perhaps no wonder that he sometimes comes across as defensive.

Lee can dish it out too, and one such target in *Bamboozled* is fashion designer Tommy Hilfiger,[32]

---

32. In his DVD commentary, Lee recounts a funny story in which Hilfiger, after seeing the film, bumped into Lee on the street. Lee affects a whimpering, whiny voice to impersonate Hilfiger: "'Spike, I want you to know I've done so much for black people. Oh Spike, how could you do this? I've been giving money to the Martin Luther King fund. Every summer I send ghetto black kids to camp.'" Lee continues: "I was waiting for him to say 'Spike: I'm blacker than you!' … People thought

amusingly reimagined as "Timmi Hillnigger" in another faux-commercial, this time for an "urban" clothing line aggressively marketed to black youth. "Hillnigger" (Danny Hoch) is a toothsome white entrepreneur who appears in front of a bevy of gyrating black and Latino women and scowling homeboys, with the Brooklyn Bridge looming in the background. He's an outrageous parody of wiggerdom, spouting a marble-mouthed mangling of black vernacular—"My name be Timmi Hillnigger. I was born up in STRONG Island, so you know I be knowing my peeps, my niggas in the GEE-TO!" Lee gives Hillnigger some of the most unsubtle dialogue ever committed to film, just in case the viewer isn't getting the message: "If you wanna keep it really real, never get out of the GEE-TO, stay broke and continue to add to my multimillion dollar corporation, keep buying all my gear. We keep it so real, we give you the bullet holes!"

It's another unambiguous depiction of neo-minstrelsy: an empowered white middle-class male getting rich off the back of black people, while minority performers debase themselves onscreen for a quick buck. And yet Lee comes perilously close here to displaying a distinct lack of self-awareness: regardless of the aesthetic qualities of his own famed Nike commercials with Michael Jordan (yes, they are better, subtler, and less aggressively cynical), he

---

I was attacking Jesus Christ himself. 'How could you say that about Tommy?' It was so easy to turn Hilfiger into Hillnigger."

too has played a significant role in the commodification and fetishization of high-end sports apparel for young consumers. While the Hillnigger commercial is unarguably one of the film's funniest sequences, and its parodic style fiendishly accurate, its inclusion leaves Lee looking somewhat truculent. It is, however, fully in keeping with the film's scorched earth approach.

Bamboozled's main narrative concludes in depressing fashion, with the assassination of Manray by the Mau Maus, their subsequent massacre by the police, and Sloan's slaying of Delacroix. Writing in *Cineaste*, Greg Tate, while broadly supportive of the film, argued that Lee copped out by failing to "confront the film's true source of evil—not the minstrel mask but that of corporate white supremacy." I understand Tate's perspective—it would have been far less wretched to see Sloan attempt to cut off the head of the snake. Yet her decision to kill the pathetic Delacroix rather than Dunwitty simply underlines the dispensability of characters like him within intractable, unbreakable corporate obelisks whose currency, argues Lee, is the maintenance of stereotypes and the perpetuation of white supremacy in vital creative positions. She, too, has effectively been bamboozled. As such, the conclusion of the narrative is entirely and sensibly reflective of the dark emotional and psychological place from which Lee so evidently conceived the film.

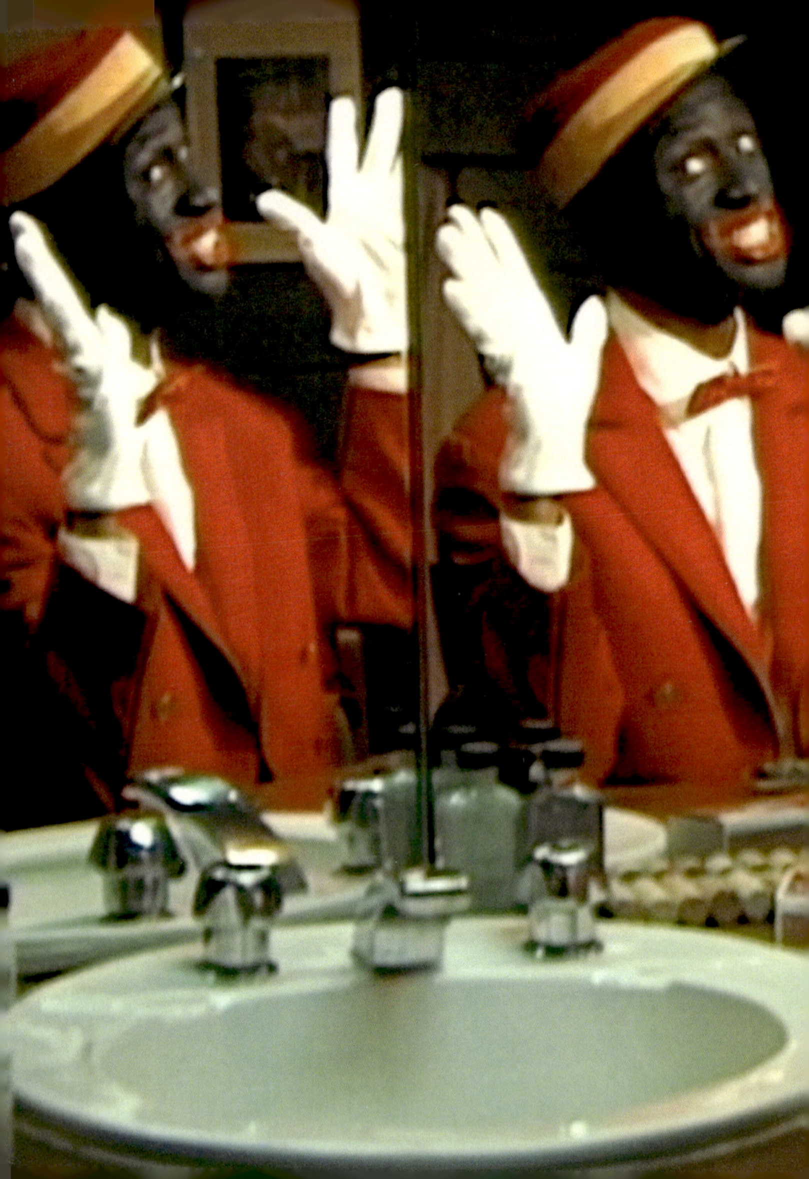

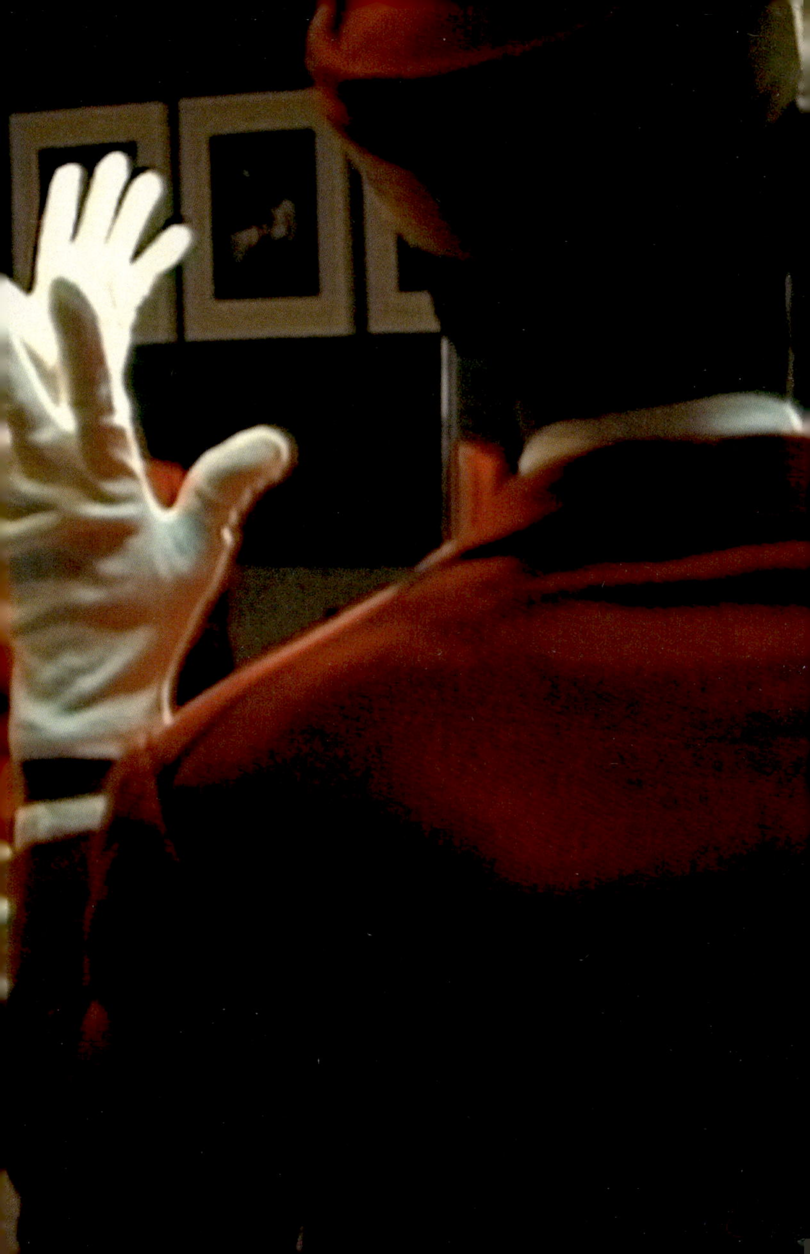

A Storm of Denigration: The Horror of Minstrelsy

In *Bamboozled*, Spike Lee, making hay in his inimitably cascading pop style, characterizes minstrelsy as something akin to an abstract virus; a malevolent mainstay on the continuum of black representational degradation. Like the voracious bug in John Carpenter's *The Thing* (1982), minstrelsy, argues Lee, simply requires a host to thrive. Such "hosts" pepper the film's landscape, from poor, confused Delacroix, with his tragic and destructive act of compromised "whiteness," to the rambunctious, institutionally-empowered wiggery of Dunwitty, to the powder keg posturing of the Mau Maus.

However its most prominent and unfortunate "hosts" are the men who wind up parading themselves, burnt cork style, on prime time television: Manray and Womack. The former is played by Savion Glover, a professional dancer in his first major film role, while the latter is incarnated by Tommy Davidson, a comic who, like Damon Wayans, came to prominence on *In Living Color*. The casting of non-stars by Lee and casting director Aisha Coley is a masterstroke—their relative unfamiliarity allows the viewer more space to project complex thoughts onto them, while they use their respective skills to highlight a painful central paradox of theatrical minstrelsy: just because the end result is a debasing visual spectacle, it doesn't negate the talent that goes into making it happen.

In *The New Millennium Minstrel Show*, Lee wisely, and bravely, allows Glover the room to be a superb dancer, and

Davidson the space to display his quick wit and oratorical felicity against the backdrop of Victor Kempster's imaginative production design—its most strikingly horrible element is a gaping sambo mouth from which the performers emerge. The routines draw on many historical influences, from *Amos and Andy*-esque clowning to a bit known as "indefinite talk"— well known from the all-black Hollywood musical *Stormy Weather* (1943)—in which the men, with deft comic timing, keep interrupting each other, prematurely responding to the information they've just cut off.

Some of these sequences go on just long enough for the viewer to become submerged in their art and *almost* forget about the blackface. In one fantastically inane routine, Davidson, in full country boy coon mode as Sleep n' Eat, manically and repeatedly sings "You ain't never seen no niggers getting down like this, getting down with a fiddle," while a fulsome country hoedown builds steam behind him. Lee cuts to Delacroix, with his guard down, screaming with laughter at the routine, and then to the Mau Maus' studio, where one member, much to the disgust of his colleagues, is also cracking up. ("This shit is funny to me, son," he harrumphs to a roomful of murderous glares). I must confess, I laughed too. Lee understands that the convulsion of unexpected laughter is indivisible from the pain and shame of the whole spectacle. It's one of *Bamboozled*'s most profound truths.

The show's ebullient public face—or mask—is, however, afforded an unbearable pathos by the scenes in which the men

A Storm of Denigration: The Horror of Minstrelsy

are depicted backstage, isolated in separate dressing rooms, applying their make-up, while Blanchard's score ebbs softly in the background. Lee lingers on the procedural elements, with disturbing close-ups of the burning and mixing of the cork paste intercut with disorienting, multiple-reflection shots of the men staring into harshly-lit mirrors. The pervasive aura of pain in these desolate sequences is only intensified by the addition of Sloan's ostensibly soothing instructional voiceover: "We should do it like they did in the day ... Please put cocoa butter on your face and hands to protect your skin," she coos, softly. But this is merely physical protection: it's infinitely harder to protect the soul.

The process of applying the make-up genuinely brought Davidson to tears, and his wet, glistening eyes, shining out from under his artificially blackened skin, make the final cut, with devastating effect. In *The Making of Bamboozled*, he says: "It was emotional. It brought out feelings, for me as a black person, how low we had to stoop to survive. Putting on the blackface and all that stuff was just a way of eating, a way of getting your family fed. Put it this way: we already in blackface, we ain't gonna get any blacker. It was just putting us down more."

Throughout, Lee is careful to draw sharp distinctions between the two performers. Though they are both motivated by a similar combination of money and a desire to entertain ("I'm just happy to be hoofin' and gettin' paid for it," says Manray), Womack is skeptical from the off, and Davidson's sad, watchful eyes convey the sense of a man carefully measuring financial reward against potential spiritual debasement. Manray, however, has a laddish, naive rapacity which marks him out immediately as an endangered species; he's like a male ingénue from Hollywood of yore. Manray is completely disinterested when Sloan, late in the film, attempts to explain to him, as a cautionary tale, the career and compromises of the legendary black Vaudevillian Bert Williams,[33] whom American comic W. C. Fields once described as "the funniest man I ever saw and the saddest man I ever knew." Instead, he just wants to get jiggy.

Manray works hard, though, and Lee is careful to highlight that his talent isn't simply natural and magical: his skills are the result of hours of practice—a pointed contrast to the depiction of his minstrel show character, and so many other black stereotypes throughout history,

---

33. Bert Williams was the star of the first ever all-black-cast American feature (1913), unmarked reels of which were found by staff of New York's MoMA, who subsequently named it *Lime Kiln Club Field Day*. Williams was the only cast member to appear in blackface. I interviewed curator Ron Magliozzi, and he told me that *The Birth of a Nation*'s success was a determining factor in keeping Williams' film from ever coming out. He said: "I believe *Birth* changed everything. The film [in our exhibition] was trying to compete in the market of what comedy films looked like in the period, and to highlight how good the performances were." Instead, only the films that featured Williams in stereotyped "coon" roles saw the light of day. "The film they didn't release wasn't racist enough; the films they did release [*Fish* and *Natural Born Gambler*, both in 1916] were."

A Storm of Denigration: The Horror of Minstrelsy

as a shiftless layabout. Manray is depicted as being fiercely demanding of his fellow cast members in a New York rehearsal space: "How old are you? 10? You wanna live to see 11?" he snaps at the small child who plays "Little Nigger Jim." Manray's exacting approach is the tipping point for Womack, and it prompts the pair to argue. After Manray has belittled Womack's contribution to the duo, Womack makes his opinion clear: "New Millennium, huh? Same bullshit, just done over." He turns his hand over his face, says "I tap dance for you massa, I coon for ya, anything to make you laugh," and slopes away sadly, out of frame. It's a low-key exit, but Womack's display of dignity and defiance constitutes the film's most uplifting moment.[34]

There's a third minstrel man in *Bamboozled*, and he shouldn't be forgotten: the opportunistic MC Honeycutt, dazzlingly portrayed by the wizened Thomas Jefferson Byrd. Byrd has vividly essayed myriad ne'er-do-wells for Lee (an AIDS-addled junkie in *Clockers* [1995]; a seedy,

---

34. William A. Graham's brilliant, compassionate, and criminally underseen TV film *Minstrel Man* (1977) is a fascinating complementary text for *Bamboozled*. It follows two black brothers in a traveling minstrel show in the early 1900s. The older brother Harry (Glynn Turman) is determined to succeed in a field that is dominated by white performers in blackface; the younger, Rennie (Stanley Bennett Clay), is a composer fighting to break away from the stereotypes associated with black minstrel performers. Rennie's quest for integrity, whatever the cost— and it is a severe cost, as the film's tragic ending shows—makes him analogous to Junebug and, ultimately, Womack.

violent pimp in *He Got Game* [1998]; a throaty pastor in *Da Sweet Blood of Jesus* [2014]), but he's never been better than he is in *Bamboozled*, where his lascivious tones and lanky physicality fuel his slippery aura. He is first spotted in the audition scene, where he charms Delacroix et al. with an idiosyncratic, self-aware spin on the minstrel tradition ("Do blackface and a monkey shine, cut a jig at the same time") and a telling update on Shakespeare: "To be or not to be? That's the motherfucking question." That is, indeed, the motherfucking question, and he—like Manray and Womack—opts "to be."

Following the departure of Womack late in the film, Honeycutt enthusiastically assumes a more involved role in the *Mantan* production. In the final minstrel show scene, we find him onstage, dressed as a dolled-up, glitter-encrusted "Honest" Abraham Lincoln, engaging an expectant crowd—all of whom are wearing blackface make-up—in a ghastly call-and-response routine. "Is you a nigga?" he asks: a Puerto Rican man answers in the affirmative, as does another man, who stands up to declare: "I'm a Sicilian nigga, which means I'm more of a nigga than any nigga in here. You know what they say about Sicilians. We're darker than most niggas. Bigger. And we rap better."[35]

---

35. This reference to Sicilian "niggas" is likely a pointed jab at another infamous Tarantino indulgence of the term. His screenplay for *True Romance* (1993) includes a lengthy dialogue between soon-to-be-murdered Clifford Worley (Dennis Hopper) and Italian mobster

A Storm of Denigration: The Horror of Minstrelsy

This parade of abjection coincides with Mantan's growing rejection of the whole spectacle—Lee cuts to him backstage, looking aggrieved. Honeycutt talks to a black woman, and asks her the same question: she replies with a sonorous tune—"I'm keepin' it real… a real negress"—before Honeycutt concludes with the deathless mini-soliloquy: "We are all God's niggas—even the lost souls who don't know that they niggas! They niggas too… Do you know why? Because niggas is a beautiful thang." At this point Honeycutt's eyes roll back in his head, as if he's slipped into a grotesque erotic reverie—it's one of *Bamboozled*'s most indelible images, captured by Lee in queasy close-up. Honeycutt, then, becomes a key figure in this twisted, lurid, public perversion of the time-honored black-is-beautiful credo: a "post-racial" cataclysm which relegates blackness to a dismal punchline, a fetish object.

While the younger pair Manray and Womack are actively wooed with big company bucks, for Honeycutt the opportunity is more of a leap into the unknown. We're never given his backstory, but perhaps we can read him as a thematic foil of Delacroix's father Junebug, whose unbending integrity has led to a combination of low-key

---

Vincenzo Coccotti (Christopher Walken). "Sicilians have nigger blood pumpin' through their hearts," says Worley, "If you don't believe me, look it up … Your great, great, great, great, great-grandmother was fucked by a nigger, and had a half-nigger kid. That is a fact. Now tell me, am I lyin'?"

success, moderate spiritual nourishment, and apparent alcoholism. Maybe the evidently talented Honeycutt played it straight like Junebug for many years, and simply got fed up waiting for his big break?

Though he appears only briefly, the snappily-dressed Junebug is an equally fascinating character, and his presence offers a window into complicated ideas around race and spectatorship. Junebug performs for almost exclusively black audiences in small clubs, which frees him to riff openly on white supremacy—and crack some absolutely filthy, race-themed jokes—without fear of censure or making white liberals feel guilty: put simply, his audience *gets* him. His style allies him with the ribald, black comedian stars of Lee's documentary *The Original Kings of Comedy*—Steve Harvey, Cedric the Entertainer, D. L. Hughley, and the late Bernie Mac—which came out three months before *Bamboozled* and was a smash hit with black audiences across America. Interviewing Lee, *Salon*'s Michael Sragow made the point that "*Bamboozled* protests the paucity of blacks in mainstream media, while *The Original Kings of Comedy* shows that talented black performers can operate beneath the radar of mainstream media and still be huge." Lee's response was telling: "The gatekeepers were not paying attention. I mean, the Original Kings of Comedy were selling out arenas, not dumpy little comedy clubs; they were filling 20,000 seats. And they still weren't being reviewed. They were totally ignored."

A Storm of Denigration: The Horror of Minstrelsy

Lee deserves credit for slowing down the film's pace to allow the viewer a luxurious stretch in the presence of Junebug's hilarious act. Listen closely, and he dispenses some wise and painful observations which pre-emptively expose the shallowness of Honeycutt's staged banalities: "The black man is the most copied person on this planet—everybody wanna be a nigga but nobody wanna be a nigga," and, "I hope they start hanging niggas again, then we'll find out who's black."

Versions of these sentiments went viral on social media in the aftermaths of the brutal 2014 police killings of Michael Brown in Ferguson and Eric Garner in Staten Island. Many young people justifiably wanted to know why otherwise outspoken pop stars like Justin Bieber, Miley Cyrus, and the ridiculous white Australian rapper Iggy Azalea—all of whom are happy to shamelessly appropriate black culture for their image and music—remained silent on such incidents instead of using their influence to publicly call out anti-black police brutality.

Junebug is played by the bone-dry Paul Mooney, a one-time associate of Redd Foxx and Richard Pryor who later reached new audiences with his recurring appearances as the saturnine "Ask A Black Dude" guy on Dave Chappelle's brilliant, boundary-pushing *Chappelle's Show* (2003-6). The fragile dynamics of race and spectatorship made headlines when Chappelle abruptly walked away from the show in 2006, citing the fact that a white crew member laughed at the "wrong" part of the joke during a sketch in which Chappelle appeared, in blackface, as stereotype-skewering "racial pixie"—this complex and sad situation almost sounds like a *Bamboozled* plot point. "I want to make sure I'm dancing and not shuffling," he told *Time* magazine, echoing the quest for self-determination that ultimately eludes Manray, but not Womack.

* * *

Bamboozled is, in many ways, a horror film. There are no masked, knife-wielding killers or bloodied damsels sprinting down country roads, even though events do conclude with a prolonged explosion of graphic violence. (*Bamboozled*'s violence, however, is not thrillingly cathartic in the *grand guignol* vein of the bloodbath in Martin Scorsese's *Taxi Driver*; it's more like the pustular seepage from a lanced boil, further deglamorized by the dull digital visuals.) The insidious presence of the aforementioned minstrelsy "virus" works in tandem with film's ghost-in-the-machine form—it plays like it's being shot and edited by some kind of surveillant sprite—and the increasingly hard-to-stomach presence of grotesque racist imagery, to conjure a lucidly nightmarish spell.

There's even something chilling about the way Manray and Womack are drawn into their situation in the first place. We glimpse them briefly, at the start of the film,

A Storm of Denigration: The Horror of Minstrelsy

attempting to curry favor with Delacroix at the foot of CNS HQ: he brushes them off, graciously yet firmly. Soon after, they are brusquely evicted from their squat in a police raid. Images of the eviction are cross-cut with shots of Delacroix and Sloan asleep, in separate beds, in their respective apartments. The scenes are impressionistically cut to suggest that the noise of the eviction wakes Delacroix and Sloan up with a start, at the same time, even though they are nowhere near the location of the eviction, or each other. In split-screen, they both shout "MANRAY!"—a eureka moment—down the phone to each other. This surreal, uncanny sequence is the crucible for the forthcoming nightmare, and is presented by Lee as a subconscious revelation: the talent to be exploited was under the network's noses the whole time. Yes, it's complicated—perhaps *Bamboozled* would be an easier film to parse or stomach, or its satire more crystalline, if the exploiters were all white, or if the Mantan and Sleep n' Eat roles were played by white actors blacking up.

Sigmund Freud described the uncanny as "that class of the frightening which leads back to what is known of old and long familiar," a description grimly apposite to *Bamboozled*'s tone and subject matter: we know precisely where its horror comes from—it's no secret, but it has been effectively suppressed in popular culture and histories. In *The Making of Bamboozled*, researcher Judy Aley, a white lady presumably holding solid liberal values, explains how during her process, "it was amazing to find how much [blackface footage] there is. It was amazing for me to go back and look at films that maybe I'd seen when I was a teenager that I didn't even remember had blackface sequences." This statement conveys how blackface became normalized and embedded into mainstream entertainment, and subsequently escaped the critical gaze of potentially sympathetic white viewers.

Yet in the same documentary, the African American cultural historian Clyde Taylor poetically elucidates the flipside for young black viewers, who didn't have the luxury of ignoring what they saw. He says, of watching blackface sequences in Hollywood films with his friends: "You're in an island, and then all of a sudden the storm of black denigration would come across us, and we'd duck, and wait till it was all over. We'd giggle, but we'd giggle out of self-anxiety."

Bamboozled's own storm of black denigration arrives in its staggering final montage of racially offensive imagery,[36] which is scored by Blanchard's simple, liltingly sad theme music, now fleshed out with fuller instrumentation for greater dramatic effect. By bolting together images of black and blacked-up white performers from comedies,

---

36. According to www.banned-cartoons.com, Warner Bros. denied Lee permission to include images of Bugs Bunny in Jolson-style blackface from the wartime cartoon *Any Bonds Today* (1942).

dramas, cartoons and musicals from multiple eras, Lee might be accused of lacking nuance; of eliding the complex industrial, personal and political factors informing each distinct performance. Yet the risk is worth taking. With this sequence Lee adopts the most effective possible rhetorical strategy to convey his argument that this entire body of material—this rank, roiling mass of stereotypes, presented as innocuous, harmless fun—in fact represents a collective and sustained assault on black dignity: the simplification and infantilization of black life for the consumption of mass audiences. The montage would be powerful enough viewed in isolation, but its galling poignancy is intensified by the fact that its understated presentation directly follows a narrative distinguished by excess and choleric rage.

There are many reasons why historical films like *12 Years a Slave* (2013) and *Selma* (2014) win awards and make big money at the box office. They are handsomely-made, well-acted and intellectually engaging. Crucially though, they are set at a safe remove from the present, and thus allow audiences to despair over the injustices of history as they simultaneously congratulate themselves on how far society has come.

In *Bamboozled*'s closing montage, Lee purposefully streaks the screen with unhealed psychic scars, and demands that the viewer join the dots between the past and the present. When the final picture emerges, the viewer must sadly concede that it does not look pretty.

Bibliography

Aftab, Kaleem. *Spike Lee: That's My Story and I'm Sticking To It*. London: Faber & Faber, 2005.

Andreeva, Nellie. "Pilots 2015: The Year of Ethnic Castings—About Time or Too Much of Good Thing?" *Deadline*. http://deadline.com/2015/03/tv-pilots-ethnic-casting-trendbacklash-1201386511/, March 24, 2015 [accessed Aug 2, 2015].

Archerd, Army. "Lee has choice words for Tarantino." *Variety*. http://variety.com/1997/voices/columns/lee-has-choice-words-for-tarantino-111779698/, December 16, 1997 [accessed Aug 2, 2015].

Beatty, Paul. *The Sellout*. New York: Farrar, Strauss and Giroux, 2015.

Black, William. "How Watermelons Became a Racist Trope." *The Atlantic*. http://www.theatlantic.com/national/archive/2014/12/how-watermelons-became-a-racist-trope/383529/, Dec 8, 2014 [accessed Aug 2, 2015].

Bogle, Donald. *Toms, Coons, Mulattoes, Mammies, & Bucks: An Interpretive History of Blacks in American Films*. (Fourth Edition) New York: Continuum, 2001.

Branch, Chris. "Michael Rapaport Fires Back At 'Shit Stain' Spike Lee: Say It To My Face." *The Huffington Post*. http://www.huffingtonpost.com/2014/07/22/michael-rapaportspike-lee_n_5610486.html, 22 July, 2014 [accessed Aug 2, 2015].

Clark, Ashley. "Deride The Lightning: assessing The Birth of a Nation 100 years on." *The Guardian*. http://www.theguardian.com/film/2015/mar/05/birth-of-anation-100-year-anniversary-racism-cinema, March 5, 2015 [accessed Aug 2, 2015].

Clark, Ashley. "Back to black: the 101-year making of the oldest black American starring feature." *Sight & Sound*. http://www.bfi.org.uk/news-opinion/sight-sound-magazine/features/back-black-101-year-making-oldest-black-americanstarring-feature, December 18, 2014 [accessed Aug 2, 2015].

Clark, Ashley. "Malcolm X: Spike Lee's biopic is still absolutely necessary." *The Guardian*. http://www.theguardian.com/us-news/2015/feb/19/malcolm-x-spike-lee-biopic-black-cinema-selma-the-butler, February 19, 2015 [accessed Aug 2, 2015].

Coates, Ta-Nehisi. "The Case for Reparations." *The Atlantic*. http://www.theatlantic.com/features/archive/2014/05/the-caseforreparations/361631/, June 2014 issue [accessed Aug 2, 2015].

Colapinto, John. "Barack Changes Everything." *The Guardian*. http://www.theguardian.com/film/2009/jan/04/spike-leeinterview-john-colapinto, January 3, 2009 [accessed Aug 2, 2015].

Crowdus, Gary and Dan Georgatos. "Thinking About The Power of Images." *Cineaste*, Vol. XXVI No. 2 (2001): 4-9.

D'Addario, Daniel. "Alessandra Stanley's pathetic non-apology for her Shonda Rhimes 'angry black woman' review." *Salon*. http://www.salon.com/2014/09/22/alessandra_stanleys_pathetic_non_apology_for_her_shonda_rhimes_angry_black_woman_review/, September 22, 2014. [accessed Aug 2, 2015].

Davis, Curt. "Jimmy Baldwin, Honored Prophet." *People*. http://www.people.com/people/archive/article/0,,20063945,00.html, April 8, 1974 [accessed Aug 2, 2015].

Bibliography

Davis, Ennis. "Keeping the Memory of the Chitlin Circuit Alive" *The Jaxson Mag*. https://www.thejaxsonmag.com/article/keeping-the-memory-of-the-chitlin-circuit-alive/, July 3, 2020 [accessed Jun 26 2022].

Davis, Zeinabu irene. "'Beautiful-Ugly' Blackface: An Esthetic Appreciation of Bamboozled." *Cineaste*, Vol. XXVI No. 2 (2001): 16-17.

Ebert, Roger. "Bamboozled." *RogerEbert.com* [initially *Chicago Sun-Times*.] http://www.rogerebert.com/reviews/bamboozled-2000, October 6, 2000 [accessed Aug 2, 2015].

Ebert, Roger. "Danson's Racist 'Humor' Appals Crowd At Roast." *RogerEbert.com* [initially *Chicago Sun-Times*.] http://www.rogerebert.com/rogers-journal/dansons-racisthumor-appalls-crowd-at-roast, October 10, 1993 [accessed Aug 2, 2015].

Edelstein, David. "Massa Disaster." *Slate*. http://www.slate.com/articles/arts/movies/2000/10/massa_disaster.html, October 6, 2000 [accessed Aug 2, 2015].

Farley, Christopher John. "Chappelle Speaks." *Time*. http://content.time.com/time/magazine/article/0,9171,1061512,00.html May 14, 2005 [accessed Aug 2, 2015].

Fanon, Frantz. *Black Skin, White Masks*. London: Pluto, 1986.

Freud, Sigmund. "The Uncanny." http://wwwrohan.sdsu.edu/~amtower/uncanny.html, 1919 [accessed Aug 2, 2015].

Gane-McCalla, Casey. "Spike Lee Compares Tyler Perry to Amos and Andy." *News One*. http://newsone.com/191851/spike-leecompares-tyler-perry-to-amos-and-andy/, May 28, 2009 [accessed Aug 2, 2015].

Gioia, Ted. "Al Jolson: A Megastar Long Buried Under a Layer of Blackface." *The New York Times*. http://www.nytimes.com/2000/10/22/arts/22GIOI.html, October 22, 2000 [accessed Aug 2, 2015].

Goldstein, Steve, "By Any Means Necessary: Spike Lee on Video's Viability" in *Spike Lee Interviews*, edited by Cynthia Fuchs. Mississippi: University Press, 2002.

Guerrero, Ed. *Framing Blackness: The African American Image in Film*. Philadelphia: Temple University Press, 1993.

Guerrero, Ed. B*FI Modern Classics: Do The Right Thing*. London: BFI, 2001.

Guerrero, Ed. "Bamboozled: In the Mirror of Abjection" in *Contemporary Black American Cinema: Race, Gender and Sexuality in the Movies*, edited by Mia Mask. New York: Routledge, 2012.

Holden, Stephen. "FILM REVIEW; Trying On Blackface in a Flirtation With Fire." *The New York Times*. http://www.nytimes.com/movie/review?res=9C01E2D9163CF935A35753C1A9669C8B63, October 6, 2000 [accessed Aug 2, 2015].

hooks, bell. *Reel to Real*. New York: Routledge, 2009.

Bibliography

Jones, Alice. "Ridley Scott, it's not about casting 'Mohammad so-and-so', it's about realizing you have a duty to make stars of nonwhite actors." *The Independent*. http://www.independent.co.uk/voices/comment/ridley-scott-its-not-about-castingmohammad-soandso-its-about-realising-you-have-a-duty-tomake-stars-of-nonwhite-actors-9891302.html, November 28, 2014 [accessed Aug 2, 2015].

Jones, Lisa and Lee, Spike. *Do The Right Thing. A Spike Lee Joint*. New York: Simon & Schuster, 1989.

Klawans, Stuart, "Amos, Andy 'n' You." *The Nation*. http://www.thenation.com/article/amos-andy-n-you/, October 19, 2000 [accessed Aug 2, 2015].

Koresky, Michael. "Rebirth of a Nation." *Reverse Shot*. http://reverseshot.org/symposiums/entry/262/bamboozled", July 12, 2007 [accessed Aug 2, 2015].

Lane, Anthony. "Actors and Addicts." *The New Yorker*, October 9 2000: 100.

Lee, Spike. *Bamboozled* Director's Commentary. New Line Home Video, 2001. Film.

Lee, Spike and Pollard, Samuel D. dirs. *The Making of Bamboozled*. New Line Home Video, 2001. Film.

Lee, Spike with Wiley, Ralph. *By any means necessary: The trials and tribulations of the making of Malcolm X ... (while ten million motherfuckers are fucking with you!)* London: Vintage, 1993.

Levinthal, David. *Blackface*. New Mexico: Arena, 1999.

Lucia, Cynthia. "Race, Media and Money—A Critical Symposium of Spike Lee's *Bamboozled*." *Cineaste*, Vol. XXVI No. 2 (2001): 4-9.

Lumenick, Lou. "'Bamboozled' Just Brilliant: Spike Lee Takes His Sharpest Shot." *The New York Post*. http://nypost.com/2000/10/06/bamboozled-just-brilliant-spike-lee-takes-his-sharpest-shot/, October 6, 2000 [accessed Aug 2, 2015].

Lott, Eric. *Love & Theft: Blackface Minstrelsy and the American Working Class*. New York: Oxford University Press, 1993.

McGowan, Todd. *Contemporary Film Directors: Spike Lee*. Illinois: University Press, 2014.

Morrison, Toni. "Talk of the Town—Comment." *The New Yorker*. http://www.newyorker.com/magazine/1998/10/05/comment-6543, October 5 1999 issue [accessed Aug 2, 2015].

Moss, Robert. "Was Al Jolson 'Bamboozled'?" *Los Angeles Times*. http://articles.latimes.com/2000/oct/20/entertainment/ca-39153, October 20, 2000 [accessed Aug 2, 2015].

Mossman, James. "Race, Hate, Sex, and Colour: A Conversation with James Baldwin and Colin MacInnes" in *Conversations with James Baldwin*, edited by Fred R. Standley and Louis H. Pratt. Mississippi: University Press, 1989.

Bibliography

Nance, Terence. "Terence Nance (An Oversimplification of Her Beauty) Talks Ridley Scott's *Exodus: Gods and Kings*." *The Talkhouse*. http://thetalkhouse.com/film/talks/terence-nance-anoversimplification-of-her-beauty-talks-ridley-scotts-exodusgods-and-kings/, December 16, 2014 [accessed Aug 2, 2015].

Newman, Kim. "Bamboozled." http://www.empireonline.com/reviews/review.asp?fid=6745, 2001 [accessed Aug 2, 2015].

Nichols, Alex. "Diamond and Silk Run the Most Obvious Con on the Right." *The Outline*. https://theoutline.com/post/6705/diamond-and-silk-dummycrats-review, November 27, 2018 [accessed Aug 28, 2022]

Nolan, Hamilton. "Tom Hanks' Son Chet: 'Fuck Yall Hating Ass Niggaz'." *Gawker*. http://gawker.com/tom-hanks-son-chetfuck-yall-hating-ass-niggaz-1708166937, June 1, 2015 [accessed Aug 2, 2015].

O'Hehir, Andrew. "Bamboozled." *Salon*. http://www.salon.com/2000/10/06/bamboozled/, October 6, 2000 [accessed Aug 2, 2015].

Rhodan, Maya. "Rachel Dolezal Breaks Silence: 'I Identify as Black'." *Time*. http://time.com/3922477/rachel-dolezal-nbc-today-blackidentify/, June 16, 2015 [accessed Aug 2, 2015].

Ridley, John. "The Manifesto of Ascendancy for the Modern American Nigger." *Esquire*. http://www.esquire.com/newspolitics/news/a162/esq1206blackessay-108/, November 26, 2006 [accessed Aug 2, 2015].

Rogin, Michael. "Nowhere Left to Stand: The Burnt Cork Roots of Popular Culture." *Cineaste*, Vol. XXVI No. 2 (2001): 14-15.

Rosenbaum, Jonathan. "Bamboozled." *The Chicago Reader*. http://www.chicagoreader.com/chicago/bamboozled/Film?oid=1048217, 2000 [accessed Aug 2, 2015].

Samuels, Allison. "Spike's Minstrel Show" in *Spike Lee Interviews*, edited by Cynthia Fuchs. Mississippi: University Press, 2002.

Sarris, Andrew. "Spike Lee on Race and the Idiot Box." *The New York Observer*. http://observer.com/2000/10/spike-lee-on-raceand-the-idiot-box/#ixzz3hfrVdRt8, October 9, 2000 [accessed Aug 2 2015].

Schuyler, George S. *Black No More*. New York: Dover, 2011.

Sragow, Michael. "Black Like Spike" in *Spike Lee Interviews*, edited by Cynthia Fuchs. Mississippi: University Press, 2002.

Tate, Greg. "Nigs R Us, or How Blackfolk Became Fetish Objects" in *Everything But The Burden: What White People are Taking From Black Culture*, edited by Greg Tate. New York: Harlem Moon, 2003.

Tate, Greg. "*Bamboozled*: White Supremacy and a Black Way of Being Human." *Cineaste*, Vol. XXVI No. 2 (2001): 15-16.

Taubin, Amy. "Spike Lee's Own Scary Movie." *Village Voice*. http://www.villagevoice.com/film/spike-lees-own-scarymovie-6417368, October 3, 2000 [accessed Aug 2, 2015].

Taylor, Yuval, and Jake Austen. *Darkest America: Black Minstrelsy from Slavery to Hip-Hop*. New York: W.W. Norton, 2012.

Bibliography

White, Armond. "Post-Art Minstrelsy." *Cineaste*, Vol. XXVI No. 2 (2001): 12-14.

White, Armond. "More Trash by Spike Lee." *The New York Press*. http://www.nypress.com/more-trash-by-spike-lee/, October 10 2000 [accessed Aug 2, 2015].

Yang, Jeff. "The sad racial farce of Mindy Kaling's brother." *CNN*. http://www.cnn.com/2015/04/08/opinions/yang-mindykaling-brother/, April 8, 2015 [accessed Aug 2, 2015].

Younge, Gary. "Spike Lee on *Oldboy*, America's violent history and the fine art of mouthing off." *The Guardian*. http://www.theguardian.com/film/2013/dec/01/spike-leeoldboy-interview-director, December 1, 2013 [accessed Aug 2, 2015].

Zeitlin, Matthew. "Scott Rudin On Obama's Favorite Movies: 'I Bet He Likes Kevin Hart.'" *Buzzfeed*. http://www.buzzfeed.com/matthewzeitlin/scott-rudin-on-obama-i-bet-he-likes-kevinhart#.uiwX0PBZq, Dec 10, 2014 [accessed Aug 2, 2015].

Various authors. "The Best Films of the '00s." *The A.V. Club*. http://www.avclub.com/article/the-best-films-ofthe-00s-35931, Dec 3, 2009 [accessed Aug 2, 2015].

www.banned-cartoons.com

www.boxofficemojo.com

www.imdb.com

About the author

Ashley Clark is a writer and film programmer, and since 2020 has worked as the curatorial director at the Criterion Collection. Previously, he worked as director of film programming at the Brooklyn Academy of Music, and he has curated film series at BFI Southbank, the Museum of Modern Art, TIFF Bell Lightbox, and the Smithsonian National Museum of African American History & Culture, among other venues. He has contributed writing to publications including *The New York Times*, *Vulture*, *Film Comment*, *Reverse Shot*, *Sight & Sound*, and the *Guardian*. Ashley was born and raised in London, England, and now lives in Jersey City, NJ. This is his first book.

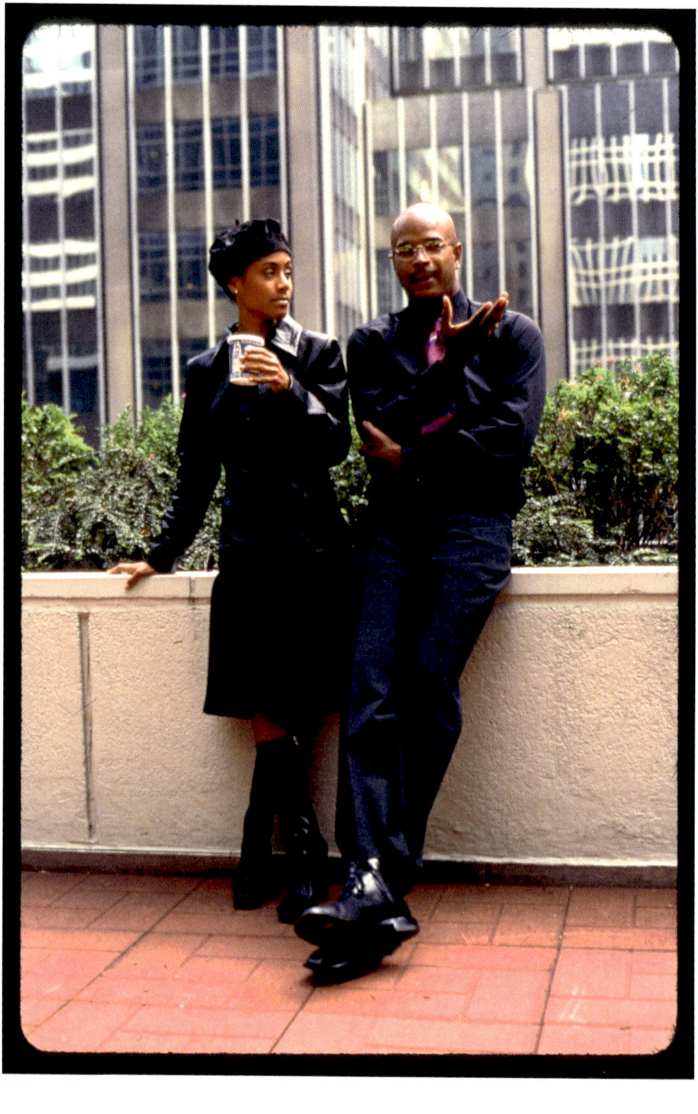